THE WILD ANIMALS OF INDIA

THE
WILD ANIMALS OF INDIA

Reprinted from the Journal of
THE BOMBAY NATURAL HISTORY SOCIETY

2016
BIOTECH BOOKS
DELHI - 110035

First Published 1934-1936
First Indian Impression 1988
Second Indian Impression 2004
Third Indian Impression, 2007

ISBN 81-7622-106-6

Published by : **BIOTECH BOOKS**
1123/74, Tri Nagar,
Delhi - 110 035
Phone: 27382765
e-mail: biotechbooks@yahoo.co.in

Showroom : 4762-63/23, Ansari Road, Darya Ganj,
New Delhi - 110 002
Phone: 23245578, 23244987

Printed at : **Chawla Offset Printers**
New Delhi - 110 052

PRINTED IN INDIA

THE VICEROY'S HOUSE.
NEW DELHI.

November 1933.

Having read with interest for many years the Journal of the Bombay Natural History Society I strongly commend to the notice of the reading public their series of articles on the Mammals of the Indian Empire.

The whole purpose of these articles is, as I understand it, to increase interest in all the wild life of the country with a view to ensure that necessary steps will be taken to prevent the wholesale destruction of our wild animals.

When I call to mind the vast areas in Canada (where I lived for four happy years) which are set aside as sanctuaries for this purpose, and realise that the same thing has been done in many other countries, I feel that more could be done in this country by reserving certain areas of our great forests in order to preserve in the future all the varied Fauna of India.

As a lover of Nature and one who can look back on many happy days spent in India's vast jungles, I trust that these articles may do much to achieve the great purpose which their wishes hope to secure.

Contents

PART I

PART II.

PART III

PART IV

THE WILD ANIMALS OF THE INDIAN EMPIRE.

PART I.

INTRODUCTION.[1]

The Preservation of Wild Life in the Indian Empire.

The purpose of the present series of articles is to give a general account of the Mammals of the Indian Empire.

For many years, the Bombay Natural History Society, through the medium of its *Journal* and other attractive publications, has endeavoured to create and stimulate in India an interest in the wild life of the country.

The necessity for this interest, particularly among our educated classes, is becoming more and more evident with the passing of time. During the past, extensive undisturbed areas of primeval forest, jungle and desert gave safe harbourage to wild creatures, and provided sure guarantee of their survival. But changing conditions in the country, the gradual conquest of forests and waste lands, above all, the building of new roads and the radical improvement in methods and rapidity of transport have left few areas in the Peninsula of India which are free from intrusion by Man. These factors have had and are continuing to have a disastrous effect on the wild life of the country. The danger to it has been accentuated in recent years by the enormous increase of firearms in use and by the inability of many of the Provincial Governments to enforce such laws as exist for the protection of wild animals.

In the past, similar conditions existed in most western countries. Forests were cut down, streams polluted and their livestock exterminated to meet the needs of the moment with no thought of the morrow. Even in tropical lands, gradually permeated with the spirit of material progress, primitive Nature has had to give way little by little to invading towns and settlements. Ruthless destruction of wild life and a prodigal wastage of natural resources have invariably preceded the establishment of material and prosperous civilization. Thus the magnificent animal life of many tropical and sub-tropical lands—and our country is no exception—has been driven to its ultimate retreat in fast diminishing forests and is to-day threatened with utter extermination.

Even the great marine animals of the sea—the whales and fur-bearing seals—have not escaped this menace of extinction. The solitudes and vast spaces of the ocean have not been able to shelter them from the rapacity of man. Like the terrestrial species, they have been subjected to ceaseless persecution, made

---

[1] An Address given by Mr. S. H. Prater, M.L.C., C.M.Z.S., the Society's Curator, at the Jubilee Meeting of the Society held in Bombay on the 10th of August, 1933.

more easy by the perfection of methods employed in the destruction of life—both human and animal.

A Changed Outlook and Some Reasons for it.

But in recent years a gradual change has developed in Man's outlook upon the Domain of Nature. This change has been brought about partly by the spread of education and enlightenment. It is engendering a growing opposition to this wanton destruction of life, however much it may profit the destroyer. It is creating the more humane conception that it is the duty of Man to see that the wild creatures of the world are not annihilated. But apart from humanity, which in itself should impel Man to grant to lesser creatures the right of existence, there are other considerations which must influence him.

The spirit of this age, with its urge for discovery and research, with its marked tendency towards the popularization of Science among the masses and the dissemination of its truths and discoveries is fostering a widespread and intelligent recognition of the immense value to man of the myriads of species, vegetable and animal, which share with him this Planet. Today there is no educated man who does not realise that the realm of Nature provides Science with a vast and productive field for research. There is none who is not impressed with the belief that such research has given and will continue to give us results of great practical and educational value.

There are numerous investigations, anatomical, physiological, ecological, geographic and evolutionary which can only be made by the study of animal life. While considerable data has been accumulated by the study of dead specimens in museums or of the living creatures in the laboratory, the 'whence, how and where' of his existence which Man is seeking to discover cannot be discovered by these means alone. The study of the living creature under the natural conditions of its natural environment is equally important.

It is also true that there are material considerations apart from scientific. We have been accustomed to look upon Beasts of Prey as creatures to be exterminated. But with a clearer understanding of the role they play in maintaining the balance of life we know now that even predatory animals have a distinct value. They are a controlling influence against over-population by species whose unchecked increase would adversely affect the interests of Man. On the other hand, there is the utilization for Man's benefit of animal products such as furs, hides and horns which in themselves represent a valuable economic asset. Furs collected from all parts of the world and assembled in London for sale during the current year were assessed at a value of £3,000,000. There is necessity for conserving the sources of supply which are not inexhaustible. Again, Science has revealed and is continuing to reveal hitherto undreamed of possibilities in the uses of animal products and their employment in the treatment of human debility and disease. Who can say what products still remain to be discovered which will one day be of priceless value to Man? Finally the wild life of a country is a source of sport and enjoyment to its people—It gives healthy recreation to all classes and is a constant attraction to visitors. It is also a definite source of income to the State because of the revenues realised from the sale of shooting licenses and on the imports of sporting arms and ammunition. But obviously it is also an asset which may vanish without reasonable efforts for its conservation. For these and other reasons, it is now admitted generally, both in Europe and America, that the natural beauties of a country, its varied fauna and flora are an asset to its people, an asset to be protected and preserved to their own advantage and to the advantage of future generations.

What other Nations are doing to Preserve Wild Life.

It is interesting and instructive for us in India to know what other nations are doing to preserve wild life.

The movement for the protection of Nature had its origin barely 50 years ago. It is the European nations and the American people who set an example to the World as to what could and ought to be done to preserve wild life within their lands. In the United States of America, the rapid development of the country, the spread of agriculture and industry threatened the destruction of its indigenous fauna. The tragedy was averted by establishing great National Parks or Reserves which not only give inviolable sanctuary to wild animals, but also offer the people an added attraction because of their scenic beauty, their historical, geographical or archaeological interest.

These National Parks provide the means by which the clash of interests between Man and the Animal is obviated; whereby security is found for the creature without imposing undue restraint upon human progress. The idea gained ground because of the people's approval. Today, in the United States, there are no less than 40 great National Parks covering more than 3 million acres of land set aside for the protection of wild life.

This magnificent effort for the protection of Nature has its parallel in the British Empire, so rich in the varied aspects of its wild life. In Canada, in New Zealand, Australia and the Union of South Africa great reserves have been created which give shelter and security to the wild life of these lands. The Kruger National Park in South Africa is the largest in the British Empire if not in the world. It covers over 8,000 square miles of territory. No park in the world contains a more marvellous assemblage of wild animals. Quite apart from the protection given to the wild life of the country, this magnificent park fully justifies its existence by way of the yearly increasing revenues it brings to the State. The effort for the conservation of wild life has been equally splendid in Canada. Here again the public response evoked by the numerous National Parks within the Dominion has resulted in bringing in a great amount of money into the country. These measures have been taken by a race of people who are keenly concerned in the progress and development of their countries and nevertheless realise the advantage of making provision to safeguard their wild life from destruction.

Within the last 20 years other nations have followed the example set by the Anglo-Saxon peoples. Switzerland has established her splendid national park amid the scenic grandeurs of the Engadine. Italy and Spain have created similar sanctuaries. Sweden surpasses all Continental countries with her 14 national parks. Finland and Austria have established numerous reserves for the protection of wild animals. Poland and Czecho-Slovakia have created a common park on their frontiers in the region of Tatara and thus incidentally, in a common desire for the protection of Nature, they have found a happy solution of a vexed territorial problem. Belgium, if not the first in the field, has been equally energetic. The great wild life sanctuary in the Belgian Congo, known as the Parc National Albert, was created by Royal Decree in 1925 and by 1929 increased tenfold in area. Five hundred thousand acres of mountain and forest have been set apart for the protection of African wild life. This great reserve is open to the students of the world and in the years to come it will prove of inestimable value to scientists and to all who love Nature and are interested in it.

The cause of conservation has been advanced also by various International Conferences the last of which was held in Paris in 1930. In 1900, the British Government convened a conference in London of the representatives of the Powers which resulted in the London Convention for the Preservation of Animals, Birds and Fish in Africa. It was signed by the Plenipotentiaries of Great Britain, France, Germany, Belgium, Italy, Spain and Portugal, and is described as the Magna Charta of wild life in Africa. In 1913 an International Conference for the Protection of Nature was held at Berne at which 17 Governments were represented. The principal conclusions of this Conference was the decision to establish a central organization to deal with the question of Wild Life Preservation on an international basis. The war made this impossible and it was not till 1928 that the recommendations of the Berne Conference were given effect. A central Bureau, designed to develop as the pivot of an international movement for the protection of wild life was established at Brussels. It is known as the 'International Office for the Protection of Nature'.

Similarly, within the British Empire, the London Conference resulted in the foundation of the Society for the Preservation of the Fauna of the Empire, which has given a great impetus to the movement in England and the Colonies and has now for many years exercised its great influence in the promotion of all forms of wild life protection. Reference must also be made to the American Committee for International Wild Life Protection, representing a unity of the large museums in the United States and to the Dutch Society for International Wild Life Protection.

It will be seen from what has been written that in all civilized countries there is a general recognition of the need for concerted and practical measures to stop the forces of destruction which threaten wild life in all parts of the world. There is in India, too, the gravest need for such concerted action.

India's Wonderful Fauna.

In its Fauna and Flora, Nature has endowed India with a magnificent asset. An asset which cannot fail to be generally appreciated by its people if they were led to know something of its worth and interest.

All those reasons which have made the people of western countries strive for the protection of Nature within their borders apply with just as much if not more force to our country. Its wild life, in its interest, its beauty and its marvellous variety, compares favourably with that of any country in the world. There are more than 500 different species of mammals found within the Indian Empire. They include the Elephant associated in India from time immemorial with the splendour of her princely pageantry, the Gaur or Indian Bison, the largest of existing bovines, the Great Indian Rhinoceros, the greatest of all the rhinos now inhabiting the world, the gigantic wild sheep of the Himalayas, probably the largest of their race, the Swamp Deer, the Thamin and the Spotted Deer, one of the most beautiful of all deer and the Nilghai, the Four-horned Antelope and Indian Antelope or Black Buck the only representatives of these genera. The beasts of prey include the Lion and the Tiger, the most magnificent of all the great cats, and such splendid creatures as the Clouded Leopard, the Ounce and the Marbled Cat. Other species, like our Himalayan foxes, martens, gorgeous flying squirrels and silky-haired langurs are remarkable for the beauty and value of their fur. The Musk Deer and the Civets provide the musk of commerce. Other species are remarkable for the beauty of their colouring. Our little Painted Bat (*Kerivoula picta*) with its brilliant vermilion and black wings, is, without exception, the most vividly coloured mammal in the world. Peculiarity in form and structure is displayed by that strange creature the Flying Lemur, which is neither lemur nor bat but which bears the same relationship to the shrews as the flying squirrel does to the squirrels, or by the Scaly Ant-eater which, with its long scaly body, looks more like a reptile than any form of mammal. Apart from the interest in their symmetry of form, largeness of size, beauty of colouring or strangeness of structure or habits there is always that attraction and charm which the presence of wild life gives to our forests and plains—so dear to the many that live for the out-door life.

A further interest attaches to our wild life from its association with the folk-lore and the legendary beliefs of the country. It is an interest not confined to India alone, but which has spread among men of culture everywhere because of the esteem and admiration in which her Sacred Books and writings are held.

Some 30 different mammals are mentioned by name in the *Samhitas* (i.e. the four principal Vedas). Among them is the Elephant, the favourite of Indra, whose sanctity is enhanced by the belief that eight elephants guard the eight celestial points of the compass. The Langur or Hanuman Monkey is held in veneration, as is commonly known, because of its association with other warrior monkeys who helped Rama in his campaign against Ravana. The

Lion is one of the many incarnations of Vishnu; the Tiger finds mention in the later Vedic texts. The Mungoose figures in the *Mahabharata* as a teacher of wisdom to King Yudhisthira. The Deer is always associated with Brahma, the Creator and is the constant companion of the god Mahadeva. The Wild Boar is referred to as the 'Boar of Heaven'. It is told how in the primordial floods Vishnu, taking the form of a boar, raised the submerged earth from the waters and supported it on his tusks. One could cite many more references from the Sacred Books concerning the animal life of the country. But apart from this, it is of much interest for us to know that the earliest known record of measures taken for the protection of animal life comes from India. The earliest record, which we possess today, is the Fifth Pillar Edict of Asoka by which game and fishery laws were introduced into northern India in the third century B.C. In this inscription, the Emperor had carved on enduring stone a list of birds, beasts, fishes and possibly even insects which were to be strictly preserved. The mammals named are 'Bats, Monkeys, Rhinoceros, Porcupines, Tree Squirrels, *Bara singha* = Stags, Brahminy Bulls, and all four-footed animals which were not utilised or eaten'. The edict further ordains 'that forests must not be burned, either for mischief or to destroy living creatures'.

Centuries later, the Moghul Emperors, sportsmen, men of action and born observers that they were, displayed a deep interest in the animal life of the country. Their writings are full of descriptions, some in great detail, of the animals, the plants and flowers of the country over which they ruled. While Babur, Humayun, the great Akbar and Aurangzeeb display in their writings their great love of Nature, Jehangir was a born naturalist. It is said of him that had he been the head of a great Natural History Museum instead of being the Emperor of India, he would have been a better and happier man. His profuse and engrossing memoirs are a real Natural History of the animal life of India.

The Problem of Wild Life Protection in India.

We have endeavoured to show how great an asset to our country is its wild life and to give the many reasons why we should do everything for its protection. But for the protection given to the Lion in Junaghad State and the Great Indian Rhinoceros in Nepal and Assam these two interesting animals would have been exterminated long ago. The Cheetah or Hunting Leopard, once common in Central India, is now almost extinct in the wild state. The Lesser One-horned Rhinoceros and the Asiatic Two-horned Rhinoceros, once said to be common in the grass jungles of Assam and the Sundarbans have been practically exterminated in these areas. In many districts wild animals have been totally wiped out. In others, where they were once common, they are now hopelessly depleted. One does not wish to overdraw the picture. There are parts of India where the position of wild life is still satisfactory though insecure. But equally, there are extensive areas where conditions are so appalling that, if left unchecked, they must lead to the complete destruction of all the larger wild creatures which live in them. There is yet another point which must be stressed. Any scheme for the Protection of Wild Life would be incomplete without due provision for the protection of our Birds. Quite apart from a sentimental value, birds render incalculable service to Man. While certain species may damage crops, such harm as is done by birds is overwhelmingly offset by the benefits we derive from them. Without their protection, our crops, our orchards, our food supply would be devoured or destroyed by hordes of ravaging insects. Birds are the principal agency that controls the bewildering multiplication of insect life which, if unchecked, would overwhelm all life on this planet. Birds by reason of their predominating insect food are an indispensable balancing force in Nature. The abundant bird life of this country is one of its valuable possessions. Those who appreciate its value, cannot but strive for its conservation.

If we accept this principle of Conservation as it is now accepted by almost all civilized countries, what methods must we employ to give it effect? It is obvious in a country like India, where conditions in different provinces vary so greatly, the methods of conservation must also vary, but it is necessary to arrive at some understanding of the broad principles which underlie the problem. The land may be classified for this purpose into three main categories: urban lands, agricultural lands and forest and waste lands.

Agriculture and Wild Life Protection.

As far as our wild life is concerned, one cannot expect its preservation in urban lands. Nevertheless, we believe that it is time that measures should be taken for the protection of birds in urban areas. Areas actually under the control of Municipalities or local Boards could be made, with advantage, Bird Sanctuaries, where the killing of birds should be forbidden. There is need to put an end to the wanton destruction of familiar birds which takes place in the immediate vicinity of towns.

The second category—land under cultivation—provides at once the opportunity for a clash between the interests of Man and the Animal. There are two main reasons for this. Firstly, the areas under cultivation in India are extending and will continue to extend to meet the needs of a rapidly increasing population. This has increased by 35 million within the last decade! The need of increasing the available sources of food supply can be met only by the continued absorption of waste lands or forest—the natural domain of wild life. Secondly, there is the equally imperative need of protecting these cultivated areas from wild animals. The depredations of wild animals present one of the most serious handicaps the ryot has to face. In addition to loss of cattle, there is the damage done to crops and, not uncommonly, loss of human life. Therefore, whatever the views of the protectionist, this much is clear. Human progress must continue and in the clash of interests between Man and the Animal human effort must not suffer. But this problem has been faced by other countries. Cannot a reasonable effort be made to face it in our own? That an intensive development of the agricultural resources of a country may accompany a sane and adequate policy for the conservation of its wild life is shown by the measures taken to this end by all progressive nations.

If our wild life is to find protection at all, it must find it somewhere in our forests. It is often claimed that the proximity of forests to agriculture makes them a constant source of harassment to the cultivator. If this argument is pushed to its logical conclusion, the only remedy would be to remove such protection as is now given to wild animals in our forests, for it would not be possible to remove this menace entirely, until all the large wild animals in them were killed, died of wounds or were exterminated over large areas because of their inability to breed. Surely our goal is not the total extermination of our wild life—which is what must inevitably happen unless some form of protection is given to it within its natural domain. While it is essential that the cultivator should have reasonable latitude to defend his property, it is equally essential that there should be certain areas or reserves where the shooting of animals is regulated and where the laws for their protection are rigidly enforced. Such reserves exist —roughly about one-third of British India and Burma consist of Reserved Forest—but, while we have extensive forests to shelter and laws to protect it, our wild life is everywhere on the decrease. The time has surely come when it is necessary for us to review the position and to take such measures as are necessary to give real protection to the wild life of the country. It is the opinion of some that these great State-owned forests, where laws now operate for the protection of animals, are and must continue to remain the natural sanctuaries of wild life in this country and that they would adequately fulfil the purpose of protection if they were effectively warded. The correctness of this view depends entirely on actual conditions in a particular Province. The extent and nature of the forests, their accessibility, the density of the population and the extent to which cultivation surrounds them are factors which must influence the issue. It may be found that in certain Provinces the establishment of a national park or reserve, in specially selected areas, will provide the only means of giving adequate protection to wild life without hampering agricultural development. It is certain that the creation of such a reserve or national park would give a special status to it. and thus facilitate the passing of special laws made applicable to such an area. Further, the actual selection and declaration as a National Park of certain definite areas would have the practical effect of forcing on the attention of successive generations of officials the importance of saving these areas from any danger of disafforestation and of taking all practical measures for the preservation of the wild animals found within them.

The Need for a Special Organization to Protect Wild Life.

Whether our reserve forests remain the principal sanctuaries for wild life in this country or whether in some of the Provinces the purpose is affected by establishing national parks, there is need for a real organization whose sole concern will be the protection of wild animals in these preserves. Our efforts to protect wild life have failed mainly *because of the haphazard methods we employ, the lack of any co-ordinate policy and the lack of any real protective agency to carry that policy into effect.* The Forest Department which ordinarily administers the Forest laws has multifarious duties to perform and, while the Forest Officer has discharged this trust to the best of his ability, he cannot give the question his personal attention, nor can he find time, except in a general way, to control the protection of wild life in our forests. Experience of other countries has shown the need of a separate and distinct organization whose sole concern is the protection of wild life in the areas in which it operates.

Further, the existing laws, as now applicable in many of our Provinces, are obsolete. Naturally, their primary purpose is the protection of the forest rather than its wild life. These laws require consolidation and bringing up to modern standards of conservation. No better guide to our Provincial Governments seeking to amend their game laws exists than the recently issued report of the Wild Life Commission in Malaya. Volume II of this Report gives the general principles of conservation. It shows how these principles may be embodied in an Act and indicates new administrative methods, based on actual experience and on the laws of other countries. With modifications, where necessary, it will serve as a model for Protective Legislation in India.

Lastly there is the all-important question of making adequate financial provision for carrying out the work of conservation.

In these days of depression, when most Governments are faced with deficit budgets, the apportioning of money for this purpose must be a matter of difficulty but, unless and until suitable financial provision is made by the State for the conservation of wild life within its borders, the effort cannot succeed. This much is clear. Our present haphazard methods have failed. The experience of other countries indicates the system that should replace them. The effective introduction of this system depends upon money being provided to work it. In the United States and in other countries the problem of financing the work of conservation has been helped by the creation of special funds.

The recent Wild Life Commission in Malaya, which made a careful study of this aspect of the problem, strongly urges the creation of such a fund to be termed the *Wild Life Fund* and to be used solely for the purpose of conservation. The idea is that all fees which could be collected under Wild Life Enactments, including any licenses or fees for riverine fishing, as well as revenues from all sporting arms licenses, permits, duties on arms (sporting) and ammunition (sporting) should be credited to the Wild Life Fund. If any of these fees are collected by another department, then the cost of collection should be borne by the Wild Life Fund. It is the only means by which financial provision can be made expressly for the purpose of conservation. It is the only means by which the money devoted to this purpose will have a definite relation to the revenue derived by the State from wild life sources and which, therefore, can be expended with every justification upon the conservation of these sources. It is the only way to ensure an equitable system of conservation; the only way in which a properly organised department can be stabilised. It is the solution advocated in other countries and one which is equally applicable to any country which undertakes the conservation of wild life on sound lines. If the idea of creating a Wild Life Fund is not acceptable and, if we are yet serious in our intention to do what is possible for the conservation of wild life in India, then we must replace the Wild Life Fund by an alternative policy, which will ensure the allocation of sufficient money to meet the requirements of adequate conservation. It is so easy to refuse a constructive policy and then put nothing in its place. The necessity for conservation being clear, the importance of an adequate financial policy to support it cannot be ignored.

So much for the broad outlines of the problem. They resolve themselves as we have seen into the formulation of a co-ordinate policy for the protection of Wild Life in India, into the selection of suitable areas where our wild life can be protected without undue detriment to human interests, the creation of a special agency for carrying out the work of protection and finally, a revision, wherever necessary, of such laws as exist in order to help these agencies to carry out their task effectively.

It is obvious that in a country so vast as India, with its varying climate and physical conditions, methods in conservation will vary in different provinces. The Society therefore proposes to publish a series of papers by different authors on the protection of wild life in the different Provinces of India. These articles have been written by authorities who have made a special study of the problem in the areas of which they write. Their knowledge and experience enable them to indicate exactly what measures ought to be taken for the protection of wild life and how these measures can be given effect to in a particular Province.

Those who are contributing to this instructive and helpful series are:

Central India, Mr. A. A. Dunbar Brander (late Conservator of Forests, C.P.); Southern India, Mr. R. D. Richmond (late Chief Conservator of Forests, Madras Presidency); Punjab, Mr. C. H. Donald (Director of Fisheries, Punjab); United Provinces, Mr. F. W. Champion, I.F.S. (Conservator of Forests, U.P.); Assam, Mr. A. J. W. Milroy (Conservator of Forests, Assam); Bombay Presidency, Mr. G. Monteath, I.C.S.; Burma, Mr. H. C. Smith (Honorary Game Warden, Burma); Kashmir, Capt. R. G. Wreford (Game Warden, Kashmir); Hyderabad, Mr. Salim A. Ali; Mysore, Major E. G. Pythian-Adams (Nilgiri Game Association).

We have indicated what other countries are doing for the protection of wild life but it must be apparent that the measures which they have taken, whether initiated by acts of Government or by private enterprise must owe their success to the support of public opinion. There is need for the creation of sane public opinion on the subject of wild life protection in India. At present, such opinion hardly exists and even if it does, in some quarters it may be antagonistic. This is mainly because people do not know, nor has any attempt been made to teach them something of the beauty, the interest and the value of the magnificent fauna of this country. In most western countries there is a wealth of cheap and popular literature dealing with the natural history of those lands. In India such literature as exists, is either unintelligible to the average reader or sold at a price beyond popular reach. Again, in most western countries, Nature Study teaching is a serious part of the earlier stages of the school curriculum. While its main object is to develop the child's powers of observation, it creates a love of Nature and a sense of companionship with life out of doors. It is true that in India feeble attempts are made from time to time to introduce Nature Study teaching into our Primary and Secondary schools. But often such teaching as is given, deals with pine trees and acorns, with polar bears and robin redbreasts, and has little or no relation to the child's own environment. The present series of articles is therefore written with the purpose of providing a popular and well illustrated account which will give people general information about the Mammals of the Indian Empire. Its object is to arouse interest in the Fauna of the country with a view to its protection and not its destruction. It is proposed to issue this series in six parts, dealing separately with the various orders of Mammals. While the series will appear in the Society's *Journal*, separately bound copies will be available for distribution. An important and essential feature of these articles is the large number of coloured and black and white illustrations. An attempt is being made to illustrate most of the more important species of mammals found within our limits. Our ability to undertake this expensive work is due to the generosity of Mr. F. V. Evans, a Vice-Patron of the Natural History Society and one of its most generous benefactors. He is paying for these illustrations. Mr. F. V. Evans was in fact the initiator of these articles on Wild Life Protection in India. It is a subject in which he has always interested himself and the great encouragement and very material assistance which he has given to the Society in advancing this cause must earn for him the gratitude of all those who are interested in this question. Our thanks are also due to the American Museum of Natural History, New York, and to the Field Museum, Chicago, for permission to use some of the pictures which accompany these articles. Acknowledgements are due to Mr. Pocock of the British Museum and to Mr. W. S. Millard for the help they have given in supervising the preparation of the illustrations.

The Society hopes that these articles will do something towards drawing the attention of people in India to the magnificent heritage which Nature has given them in this country. It hopes they will help them to realise the need for preserving this legacy to their own advantage and to the enjoyment of generations to come, who with the spread of education will be in a better position to appreciate its worth than we are today.

PART II.

THE DISTRIBUTION OF MAMMALS.

In the distribution of its Wild Life few regions of the Earth exceed British India in interest. The Indian Empire covering an area of approximately 1,800,000 square miles displays in its physical characters and in its temperature and climate the most remarkable variation. Its widespread frontiers include the Himalayas, soaring for thousands of feet above the level of perpetual snow, the deserts of Sind and Rajputana, the luxuriant rain swept forests of Assam and the Malabar Coast, the cold and arid plateaus of Ladak and Tibet.

Across our northern frontiers stands the chain of the loftiest mountain range in the world, while our shores are washed by an ocean which stretches south to the bleak Antarctic forming an insuperable barrier to the dispersal of our wild life.

It is proposed before describing the mammals of the Indian Empire, to give a picture of the varied conditions under which they live—these conditions being the factors which influence their distribution.

Animals are dependent directly or indirectly upon plants for their food. The vegetation of a country is therefore one of the main factors which influences the character of its animal life. But the type of vegetation, which will grow in any country, depends upon its climate and the climate upon its physical features—the level of the land, the presence or absence of mountain or hill ranges, the height and aspect of these ranges. Hence the distribution of animal life upon this Earth, as we know it today, is based entirely upon the changes which have taken place in its surface through the long ages of its history.

All through time the surface of the Earth has been changing. Mountain ranges stand in areas once submerged beneath the sea. Expanses of land have broken up to become separate continents, divided by oceans, and on the other hand dividing seas have receded to form continuous stretches of dry land.

It is believed that during the early part of the Tertiary epoch the Peninsula of India—the triangular tableland which stretches from the highlands of Central India to Cape Comorin—was a large island. This island during a still more remote period was perhaps united to Africa. But during the Tertiary period it was separated from the mainland of Asia by shallow seas which covered the plains of northern India and the whole of Kashmir. The Himalayas and the greater part of Tibet, formerly submerged beneath the sea, were then a land of moderate elevation drained by great rivers, which flowing east and west poured their alluvium and silt into the adjoining seas. During the millions of years that elapsed, while no great changes have been traced in the ancient island, the whole of those gigantic forces which created the great Himalayan ranges exerted their influence. They raised the land and drained the seas covering Assam and gave birth to the Eastern Himalayas. Thus was formed the first land connection between India and the Continent of Asia. Thus was provided a land bridge by which all the forms of life developing in Central Asia were able to enter and colonise the Indian Peninsula.

It is believed that after a great interval of time, a second upheaval took place. It produced the main Himalayan ranges and converted what was left of the intervening sea into the plains of northern India. After an epoch of quiescence, a third upheaval crumpled and ridged up a strip of this plain to form the outer ranges of the Himalayas—the group of hills known as the Siwaliks. So was formed in the course of ages the Sub-Continent of India.

What animals inhabited the country during this distant era? The remains of extinct creatures discovered in the upper layers of the Siwalik range and in other parts of the country give us a glimpse of a wonderful wealth of animal life during the Tertiary epoch. Mastodons and great herds of elephants of various species trumpeted and tramped through the swamps and reedy forests of this region. With them lived hippopotamus, rhinoceros of various kinds and a colossal four-horned ruminant the *Sivatherium*. There were troops of giraffe, of large and pigmy horses, camel, herds of wild oxen, buffalo, bison, deer, many kinds of antelope, wild pig and pig-like creatures. Further, the fossil beds reveal the existence in the Siwaliks of chimpanzees, orang-outans and baboons, of langurs and macaques. The beasts of prey included a type of cheetah or hunting-leopard, sabre-toothed tigers and various large and small felines; wolves, jackals and foxes, civets, martens, ratels and otters. The bears were represented by a species similar to our sloth bear, the rodents by various genera including bamboo rats, mole rats, porcupines and hares.

A striking fact, emerging from the comparison of the fauna of the past with that of the present, is the wonderful variety of forms which lived in those remote times and the relatively fewer forms of our day. It must be remembered that our records are incomplete. Yet we know that eleven different species of elephants and mastodons lived in the Siwaliks as compared with the solitary living form we have now. There were 6 different species of rhinoceros and several representatives of the wild boar, some of gigantic dimensions. The beasts of prey were also more numerous than those now living in that region.

This marked impoverishment of the Fauna is not peculiar to India. The remains of extinct animals unearthed in various parts of Europe, Asia and North America reveal a similar loss.

It is interesting also to note how many forms of life akin to those of that distant epoch still continue to flourish in India after millions of years. Langurs, macaques, various species of felines, hyaenas, jackals and foxes, sloth bears, ratels, mole rats, porcupines, hares, rhinoceroses, bison, and elephants allied to those which lived in the Tertiary age, still live in this country; how many again still inhabit other regions of the Earth though no longer found in India? Chimpanzees, baboons, hippopotamus and giraffes, eland, kudus and other antelope survive in Africa, though not in India. A considerable affinity has been traced between the fauna of the Siwalik period and the wild animals now living in India and Africa. Rhinoceroses, elephants, antelopes, various species of felines, hyaenas, jackals, foxes, ratels, mungooses and several forms of rodents exist in both countries. It is believed that a very large proportion of the animals which formerly existed in the Siwaliks and the allied species now inhabiting Africa and India were derived wholly or partly from the same ancestors, which may have originally migrated southward from Europe and Central Asia. The remains of extinct animals discovered in Europe and Central Asia show that elephants, rhinoceroses, hippopotami, tapirs, antelopes, lions and tigers once inhabited these regions. During this epoch it is believed that the northern countries enjoyed an almost tropical climate. But owing to a change in climate and other causes all those forms of life which were unable to adapt themselves to changing conditions perished or migrated southwards.

It is well known that during the latter part of the Tertiary Era the climate of Europe was becoming gradually cooler and that this refrigeration ended in a Glacial Epoch or 'Ice Age' in which the northern countries were subjected to an Arctic climate. The 'Ice Age' also produced glacial conditions in the Himalayan region, but whether these conditions extended into the Peninsula of India is not known.

It is assumed that all forms of life inhabiting the countries so affected were compelled to adapt themselves to the changing conditions, to migrate or perish. Some were able to react to the new conditions, many were exterminated, while others migrated southwards to colonise warmer tropical countries. Thus is explained the disappearance of numerous forms of life from the Northern Hemisphere and the Himalayas and the survival of their descendants both in India and Africa in our time.

Many forms of life, represented in the older fauna, disappeared from this country. Their place appears to have been taken by others which subsequently migrated into India from the countries lying to the east of the Bay of Bengal. Many Indo-Chinese mammals, not represented in the older Siwalik fauna, are believed to have migrated into India from the hill ranges of Assam and the countries further east. The majority of them settled in the Eastern Himalayas, while others spread through or colonised parts of the Peninsula. About 70 per cent of the mammals living in the Himalayan forests between Kashmir and Bhutan are found equally in the hill forests of Assam, Burma, South China, while some Malayan types, like the Mouse Deer and the Lorises, inhabit parts of the Peninsula. A stream of migration has also come from the West. Such species as the Indian Lion, the Indian Gazelle and the Oorial of the Punjab and Kashmir from their westerly range or their affinity with species inhabiting regions lying to the west are believed to have extended into India through her western frontiers.

Thus we see that the wild life of India is derived not only from species which were indigenous to it, which are found in no other country in the world, but also from forms, descendants of ancestors that have migrated into India from the regions which adjoin its borders. It is composed of an admixture of Indian, Malayan, Ethiopian and European elements. These foreign forms naturally predominate in parts of the country most suited to their habits. The Malayan forms abound in the damp sheltered forest clad valleys of the Eastern Himalayas and occur again with frequency in the rain swept forests of the Malabar Coast. The fauna of Kashmir, and the Higher Himalayas is marked by a predominance of European types. The main Peninsula is described as the home of the true Indian fauna. The desert tracts of Sind and the Punjab shelter an animal life somewhat uniform with that of the great Palaearctic Desert which extends westwards from Sind to the shores of northern Africa.

With this brief review of some of the factors which influenced the character and composition of the Indian fauna we may now consider its present general distribution.

India with south-eastern Asia forms part of the Oriental Region, one of the six great Zoological Realms into which the Earth has been divided to study the distribution of its animal life. Each of these Realms supports its characteristic animal life. That the animals and plants of one country or group of countries may differ from those of another must be apparent to most people. But the Indian Empire, while it forms part of the Oriental Region, presents in itself such contrasts in physical characters, such variation in climate and vegetation that its animal life naturally varies with conditions in different parts of the country.

This vast Empire has been divided into various zones or subregions each of which supports its characteristic assemblage of wild animals. There is no sharp line of demarcation between these zones. It would be difficult to plot them out exactly on a map. The animal life of one zone merges imperceptibly into that of another and there are widespread species which live in one or more zones. But on the whole it may be claimed that the animal life of a particular zone is sufficiently distinctive to be distinguishable from that of another.

The Himalayan Sub-Region.

The Himalaya Mountains, enclosed by the Indus in the West and the Brahmaputra in the East, support an animal life more or less distinct from the rest of India. But the great range of altitude of these mountains has naturally resulted in marked peculiarities of distribution in its plants and animals.

Three distinct zones, each with its characteristic assemblage of animals, are now recognised. The first covers the whole of the forested slopes of the Himalayas from the eastern frontiers of Kashmir to Bhutan. The second includes the Western Himalayas from Kashmir and eastern Ladak to Chitral, the third the arid plateaux of eastern Ladak and Tibet. The bare towering peaks above the tree line and a strip of upland grass country which lies between the main Himalayan Range and the Plateau of Tibet is regarded as a transition zone. Here the animal life of the Himalayan forests merges into one which is characteristic of Europe and Central Asia.

The foothills and lower valleys or 'dhuns' of the Forest Zone are covered with dense tropical vegetation. These lower forests are inhabited mainly by animals which are found in the forests of the Peninsula. Tiger, elephants, gaur, sambhar, and muntjac are common. In the swamps and forests of the Terai—the strip of low lying country which adjoins the foothills—gaur are replaced by buffalo, and cheetal, hog-deer and swamp-deer are found.

When an altitude between 5,000 to 6,000 feet is reached the character of the vegetation changes. The forests become dark and gloomy. Oaks, magnolias, laurels and birches covered with moss and ferns replace the sal, silk-cotton trees, and giant bamboos of the foothills. At an elevation of about 9,000 to 12,000 one enters forests of pine and fir trees, of yew and juniper with an undergrowth of scrubby rhododendrons and dwarf bamboo. We enter a temperate zone with a temperate vegetation. But there is no sharp line of demarcation between the tropical and temperate forests. The transition from one to the other is gradual; much depending on the height of the intermediate ranges and the depth of the inner valleys. In the Eastern Himalayas, exposed to the full blast of the monsoon, tropical trees reach higher levels than in the colder and drier climate of the Western Himalayas. The animal life of the temperate zone is distinguished by the absence of many species which inhabit the Indian Peninsula and by the presence of many Indo-Chinese forms, which do not occur in the Peninsula, but are common in the hill forests of Assam, Burma and Southern China. Racoons, hog-badgers, ferret-badgers, crestless porcupines, and those curious goat-antelopes the goral and the serow are some of the typical inhabitants of these temperate forests. They are not found elsewhere in India but range widely in similar forests through Assam and the countries further east. The Indo-Chinese element in the fauna is very marked in the Eastern Himalayas but, as one travels westward, it gradually disappears, until in Kashmir and the countries further west, it ceases to be the principal constituent. The probable colonization of these forests by emigrants from the hill ranges of Assam has already been commented upon.

The second great zone of the mountain system extends from Kashmir and Western Ladak to Chitral. The Indo-Chinese mammals of the Central and Eastern Himalayas are here replaced largely by Indian species and by an infusion of forms allied to European and more northern Asiatic types. Many animals living in the plains of India are or were found in this zone among them the Muntjac, the Blackbuck and the Chinkara. The Sambhar is absent. The most distinctive deer is the Kashmir Stag, a relative of the Red-Deer of Europe. Again, typically northern animals, such as the Ibex and Markhor range through these western mountains, but, like the Kashmir Stag, do not extend into the Eastern Himalayas. The Oorial or Shapu is also not found far beyond Kashmir but extends its territory westward through the Punjab, Baluchistan and Afghanistan to the Persian hill ranges. Kashmir appears then to have received its fauna from the Indian Peninsula and the countries lying to the north and west.

The bare peaks above the tree line and the strip of luscious grass country lying between the mountains and arid plateaux of Tibet is described as a transition zone—a meeting ground between the animal life of the Oriental and the northern or Palaearctic Regions. It is obvious that the huge mass of the Himalayas must be a great barrier to the free migration of animals. This obstacle combined with the great difference in climate north and south of the range has resulted in a fairly sharp line of demarcation at about the 28°, between two distinct faunas—the Oriental in the south and the Palaearctic in the north. Evidence of this is particularly marked in the Eastern Himalayas. Here north of this line live such typically northern animals as moles, water-shrews, mouse-hares, marmots, musk-deer and the bharal, while south of it, the forests are inhabited by typically Oriental animals like flying-foxes, fruit-bats, tree-shrews, civets, mungooses and Oriental squirrels.

The Tibetan Plateau together with the Eastern Ladak is regarded as a distinct faunal area. The zone does not include the low lying wooded portions of eastern Tibet but covers the barren hills and plains which lie beyond the Himalayas but within the northern frontiers of India from Kashmir to Bhutan. It is a windswept region of scanty rainfall, intense cold and high elevation and is described as the only region of the globe where desert and arctic conditions prevail. The Wild Ass, which is found in various desert parts of Asia, lives in this zone which also shelters the Arctic Hare. The Great Tibetan Sheep, the Bharal and the Yak are also typical inhabitants of these cold, desolate and barren mountains. So much for the wild life of the Himalayan Region. Its great range of altitude and variety of climate and temperature; its vegetation ranging from tropical to alpine and its geological history make it one of the most interesting zoological regions in the world.

Assam and Burma are included in the same zoological province as the forest region of the Himalayas. There is the same gradation from tropical to temperate vegetation though the purely Alpine flora of the higher Himalayas is largely absent. The distribution and character of the animal life is similar, except in Tenasserim, where the fauna is distinctly Malayan in type. These Malayan types are traceable all through the province into the hill ranges of Assam, with an intermingling of peculiar forms. Of the wild animals of Burma some, like the Gaur, are identical with those of India, others, like the Sambhar or the Thamin, are regarded as Burmese representatives of Indian forms.

THE MAIN INDIAN REGION.

India proper from the base of the Himalayas to Cape Comorin, with the exception of the Malabar Coast, is regarded as a single sub-region—the cis-Gangetic or Indian Peninsular sub-region. The northern part of this sub-region comprises the alluvial plains of the Ganges, the Indus and the Brahmaputra rivers and their tributaries. It covers the greater part of the Provinces of Assam, Bengal, Bihar, the United Provinces, the Punjab and Sind. This immense tract of level land from 90 to 300 miles wide and stretching for 1,400 miles from sea to sea separates the main Indian Peninsula from the Himalayas. South of the Gangetic Plain, the Peninsula takes the form of a triangular tableland; varying in altitude from a thousand to three thousand feet, broken up at intervals by the valleys of its intersecting rivers. The northern side of the tableland rests on confused hill ranges known collectively as the 'Vindhya Mountains'. Its two other sides are formed by the Eastern Ghats, stretching in fragmentary spurs down the Madras coast and the Western Ghats, which form the great, almost continuous, sea wall of the Bombay Presidency. The face of the triangular plateau is scarred with scattered peaks and hill ranges—outliers of the Ghats. The most notable are the Nilgiris, the Annamalais and the Pulni Hills of Southern India.

The animal life of the Indian Peninsular region is characterised by the absence of many of those Indo-chinese species which are so abundant in the hill forests of the Himalayas. It is the home of the true Indian fauna of which, the Spotted Deer, the Nilgai, the Blackbuck, the Four-Horned Antelope and the Sloth Bear are typical representatives. They are found nowhere else. Other species like the Gaur, the Sambhar and the Muntjac occur both in India and the Malay countries.

The Indian Desert Region.

The Trans-Indus districts of the Punjab, Western Sind and Baluchistan really form the eastern limits of a great desert region which extends through Persia, Mesopotamia and Arabia to the shores of North Africa. Naturally the character of the wild life of the Indian Desert region differs markedly from the rest of India. It consists mainly of species which have migrated into it from the desert lands lying beyond its borders, and of species from the Peninsula which are able to live under the conditions prevailing in these arid and sandy wastes.

The Gangetic Plain.

The general distribution of animals in the Indian Sub-Region corresponds to a large extent with the character of the vegetation which is again dependent on variations in climate and soil. In the great plain of the Ganges the rainfall is moderate and the winter temperature is correspondingly low. In the north-western portions of the Plain, in the Punjab and Western Rajputana the vegetation gradually merges into that of the adjoining desert zone. In this area live many desert forms of animals such as the desert cat, the desert fox, the desert hare and various species of desert gerbilles—colonists from the desert zone. These desert forms disappear as one travels eastwards into the more humid part of the Gangetic Plain. A feature of the dry zone of the Gangetic Plain is also the presence of large herds of antelope and gazelle. In the humid plains of Bengal, the semi-desert vegetation of the northern plain gives place to luxuriant groves of mangoes, figs and palms, such as one finds in the moist coastal tracts of the Peninsula. The wild life of this humid area differs little from that of the moister and more cultivated parts of the Peninsula. Further east, at the mouths of the Ganges, the great plain is transformed into a wilderness of swamp and forest,—the Sunderbans. It is a region of grassy savanahs and muddy islets covered with mangroves and dense evergreen forests. These forests shelter most of the larger animals found in the forests of the Peninsula with the addition of swamp-deer, buffalo, rhinoceros and such animals as have a preference for this amphibious terrain.

The Main Peninsula.

While the drainage areas of its intersecting rivers are covered with green woods and cultivation, the greater part of the tableland, which forms the main Peninsula of India, presents a scene of wide undulating plains separated by ranges of flat-topped hills. A portion of the plateau, comprising the eastern parts of Central India, Gujerat and the Deccan is sheltered from the monsoon by the great wall of the Western Ghats. It is a dry region of moderate rainfall. This dry zone extends to the low lands of the Carnatic and stretches south to the plains of southern India. These are again cut off from the monsoon by the southern hill ranges. The dry zone of the tableland has its characteristic vegetation due to climate and to soil. From the Bombay coast to the neighbourhood of Nagpur, from below Belgaum to Goona in Central India, over some 200,000 sq. miles of country, black cotton soil predominates. It is derived here from the underlying volcanic rocks known as Deccan Trap which forms the unbroken substratum throughout this area. Black soil produces its characteristic wild and cultivated vegetation. The wide grass-covered plains and the bases of the flat-topped hills in the Trap country are scattered with clumps of thorny acacias, species of *Zizyphus*, small trees and shrubs which are either leafless or burnt up in the hot weather. Forests, where they exist, are mainly deciduous and composed of stunted teak, bamboos and sundry small trees. In the open grasslands and scrub jungle, herds of gazelle and antelopes are again common. Other typical animals of the open country in the Peninsula are the Jungle Cat, the Common Fox, the Common Mongoose, the Indian Wolf, palm squirrels, hares and a variety of field rats and mice. Gaur, sambhar, spotted deer, sloth bear and wild dogs are found in its open deciduous hill forests. As one leaves the Trap country and penetrates the humid region lying north and east of Nagpur, one enters a zone where the climate is somewhat similar to the plains of Bengal, the character of the soil and of the vegetation changes. Teak ceases to be the dominant tree of the forests. It gives place gradually to Sal, while the familiar crops of the Trap country millet, pulses, and cotton yield to watery rice and cane fields. The wild life of the forests of this humid zone is enriched by the presence of wild elephants, buffalo and swamp-deer, which occur in this area.

The Malabar Coast.

The Western Ghats, in sharp contrast to the adjoining dry zone of the Deccan, presents a region of great humidity and heavy rainfall. The forests covering the western slopes are at times very dense and composed of lofty trees, festooned with numerous perennial creepers. Bamboos form a luxuriant undergrowth. In parts of the range, the forests are more open and the banks of clear streams running through them are covered with spice and betel groves.

The Nilgiris, an off-shoot of the Western Ghats, rise precipitously to form extensive grassy downs and tablelands seamed with densely forested gorges or *sholas*. They are composed of tall evergreen trees with a dense undergrowth. Sholas, similar to those of the Nilgiris, occur in the Annamallai, Pulni Hills and other South Indian ranges. They provide the main shelter to wild elephants, gaur and other large animals of these hills. The most interesting feature of the higher level forests of the Nilgiris is their affinity to the higher forests of the Assam hill ranges. Many of the trees found in these high sholas and some of the forms of animal life are common to both areas. The forests of the Western Ghats and the South Indian hill ranges have a richer fauna than the remaining areas of the Peninsular Region. Among the species limited to these forests are the Nilgiri Langur, the Lion-tailed Macaque, the Nilgiri Brown Mongoose and the Striped-necked Mongoose, the Malabar Civet and the Spiny Mouse. In the higher levels of the Nilgiris and the Annamallais are found such characteristically Himalayan animals as the Thar and the Pine-Marten.

From this general description of the composition and distribution of the mammals of the Indian Empire and of the varied conditions under which they live, it will be seen that they share with all other living things the strong natural tendency to increase their sphere of action, to extend their territory. We find animals which have originated in countries beyond our frontiers or in our northern mountain ranges extending their range and colonising the Peninsula. When a species thus spreads into a new territory, where the climate, the vegetation and the enemies it has to face are different from its original home, it must either adapt itself to these changed conditions or it will fail to establish itself. These different conditions may produce differences in its appearance and habits, in other words, produce a variation from the typical parent form. If these colonists are subsequently isolated from the parent stock by impassable barriers, produced as a result of geological and other changes, they will tend in the course of centuries to differ more and more from the parent stock. Glacial conditions which obtained in the Himalayas during the Ice Age are believed to have driven the Thar with other animals to colonise the Indian Peninsula, which is assumed to have enjoyed a more temperate climate during this epoch. The return of tropical conditions in India is believed to have resulted in the extermination of the Thar in the Peninsular Region. But those which were able to obtain a refuge in the temperate climate of the higher altitudes of the Nilgiris and Annamallai Hill ranges survived. Isolation from the parent Himalayan stock, different conditions of life, produced in the course of centuries those differences in colouring and texture of coat, shape of horn and other characters which now distinguish the Nilgiri from the Himalayan Thar. In other words, a new and distinct species was evolved. But if no impassable barriers are created, the new varieties evolved in different connected areas remain more or less alike. There is interbreeding and consequently an intergradation of characters between these varied geographical races linking them with the parent form. Thus, among many widespread species of animals, we find more or less easily distinguishable geographical races, evolved as a result of the different conditions under which they live in different areas of their range. In the case of the Gaur or Indian Bison, which extends from India through Burma and the Malay countries, there are well marked differences in the shape of the skull which enable us to differentiate between the Indian Gaur and the gaur living in the forests of the Malay Peninsula. While the Gaur of Burma and Assam intergrade between these two extreme types.

In the past naturalists were content to classify animals in accordance with the salient characters or marked differences between species. In recent years it has been recognised that it is not only necessary to classify species but it is equally or more important to systematically record geographical variations where they exist in a species. This data, when sufficiently multiplied, will in future furnish information for the investigation of problems connected with the variation and distribution of species. Therefore, in more recent publications dealing with Indian animal life, we find due attention paid to the description of geographical races wherever these occur.

It will also be seen that a knowledge of animal life gives us a better knowledge of ancient geography. It reveals changes which have taken place in the distribution of land and water and shows how the present distribution of land animals has been brought about. We have seen also some of the factors which have influenced this distribution or produced changes in or the extermination of numerous forms. In our day, the agency which accelerates these changes is Man. In India, irrigation by human agency in the desert tracts of the Punjab and Sind has resulted in the conversion of vast tracts of desert land into fertile country. This is bringing about a change in the character of the animal life of these areas. Desert species are retreating from them. They are being replaced by forms more adapted to the changed conditions. Again, Man sweeps away forests, dams rivers and wipes out of existence races of animals which are the culmination of centuries of evolution. While Man is a destructive agent, he can also become a preserver and protect wild creatures from the destructive effects of his own handiwork. The need for saving the wild creatures of this world from annihilation is recognised in most countries of the world,

Various factors, as a result of human activity, are threatening the wild creatures of India with extermination. There is, as we have seen, great need in this country for adequate measures to preserve wild life from the destruction which threatens it.

The pages which follow contain illustrations and brief descriptions of the Mammals of the Indian Empire. They are based mainly on the observations of sportsmen and Naturalists who have contributed to the pages of the *Journal* of this Society during the past 50 years, whose writings have added so much to the sum of knowledge of the Natural History of the Indian Empire.

Among other books referred to are:

Dunbar Brander, A. A. 'Wild Animals in Central India'
Evans, Major G. P. 'Big Game Shooting in Upper Burma'
Burrard, G. (Major General) 'Big Game Hunting in the Himalayas and Tibet'.
Stewart, A. E. (Col.) 'Tiger and Other Game'.
Stockley, C. H. (Lt.-Col.) 'Big Game Shooting in the Indian Empire'.
Champion, F. W. (I.F.S.) 'With a Camera in Tigerland'
,, ,, ,, 'Sunlight and Shadow in the Indian Jungle'.
Lydekker, R. 'The Great and Small Game of India'
,, ,, 'Catalogue of Ungulate Mammals (B.M.)'
Blanford, W. T. 'Fauna of British India, Mammalia'
Jerdon, T. C. 'The Mammals of India'.
British Museum, 'Game Animals of the Empire'.

PART III.

Ungulates or Hoofed Animals.

The Ungulates or hoofed animals are included in four well defined Orders of Mammals:

(1) *Proboscidea*: Elephants.
(2) *Perissodactyla*: Rhinoceros, Tapir and Horses.
(3) *Artiodactyla*: Cattle etc., Deer, Camel, Hippopotamus and Pig.
(4) *Hyracoidea*: Coneys.

All of them are ground dwelling animals, all of them exclusively or mainly vegetarians in diet. With this common mode of life there is a common general plan in their structure. Unlike the clawed limbs of beasts of prey or the grasping hands of apes and monkeys, the feet of Ungulates are unsuited to any function beyond supporting and moving the body. Their main purpose is progression. They are built to withstand rough wear and to support and carry the body with speed over long distances.

With the exception of camels and the coneys, all Ungulates have the ends of their toes encased in a large horny hoof or protected by large hoof-like nails. A few among them are clumsy and slow moving creatures. The majority are slender-limbed and fleet of foot. In the open spaces in which many of them live, speed of movement is their main protection against numerous foes.

Hoofed animals walk on the very ends of their toes, not on the soles of their feet. By this means the full extent of the limb comes into action. Its stride is increased. Now, an animal moving on the tips of its toes presents the narrowest possible portion of its body to the resisting earth. Its body obtains sufficient support and leverage. Its feet can be disentangled from the ground with greater facility. It moves with greater speed because rapid mechanical progress over the unyielding surface of the ground depends largely on one factor. The points of a moving body which come in contact with the ground must be few in number and small in area. Resistance to movement is thereby decreased. When the area presented to the ground is increased, as in the case of an animal which walks on the soles of its feet, speed is diminished. Among hoofed animals the extent of the foot coming in contact with the ground is further limited by a reduction in the number of toes. With the exception of the elephant, no Ungulate has more than four functional toes. Some have three, the majority two, horses only one. Among these animals Nature's plan has been to lengthen and strengthen the bones of one or more of the original five toes and to dispense more or less completely with the others. Coupled with this perfecting of the foot as an organ for rapid movement there is a corresponding development in the length and system of articulation of the bonelets of the wrists and ankles. These developments have given greater firmness to the foot, making it less liable 'to give' under pressure and more suited to animals which run.

Speed and surety of movement has been reached not by the immediate invention of a new limb for this purpose. Nature has availed herself of existing structures—of the normal 5-toed foot. From this she has evolved the form of limb suited to the different needs of different hoofed animals. So far as can be judged, the various hoofed animals are derived from several stocks or primitive 5-clawed ancestors. In each of them the hoofs have been independently evolved in adaptation to similar habits of life. The varied modifications which have taken place in the limbs of Ungulates is seen by comparing modern types with those which flourished in the distant past. In the instance of the Horse, a complete transition is traced from a 5-toed ungulate of the Eocene or 'Dawn Age', walking partly on the soles of its feet, to a 4-toed, then a 3-toed horse and so finally to the modern horse which has a single toe on each foot and treads the earth on the very tip of these toes. The modern horse carries the rudimentary vestiges of the second and fourth toes in the shape of 'splint bones' on each side of the long bone of its fore and hind feet. Of its first and fifth toe no trace remains.

The gradual perfecting of the fore and hind limbs as running organs in hoofed animals has been put down to the changing conditions in their environments. It is believed to be due to changes in the earth's surface, to the raising of the level of the land and the consequent change in its climate and vegetation. These changes resulted in the conversion of marshy and forested tracts into upland, open, grass-covered plains, where the safety of these animals from numerous foes now depended on their capacity for rapid flight. The same reasons are believed to explain the modifications, which took place in the course of long ages, in the teeth of Ungulates. There has been a gradual change in the shape of the teeth. An early type, still seen in man and many mammals—a type suited to a mixed or even carnivorous diet has given place to teeth with flat grinding surfaces, complicated by folds and ridges of enamel. This is seen in the molar teeth of the majority of later Ungulates. In the horse for example, the grinding surface of the cheek teeth are made up of hard enamel ridges. These ridges are braced on either side by layers of softer dentine. The massive grinding organs are thus composed of substances of different density. An effective irregular grinding surface is always maintained by the persistence of the harder enamel and the wearing away of the softer dentine. The food of the Ungulates, consisting in most cases entirely of vegetable substances which require much mastication, is believed to be the inducing cause for the complex structure of the cheek teeth in the more specialised kinds. While their grinding teeth have undergone special development there is a decided tendency among the more specialised representatives of the Order to a reduction either in the size or in the number of the front teeth. The canine teeth are frequently small or absent; while the incisor teeth in the upper jaw and more rarely both the incisors and canines in the upper and lower jaws may be wanting. All the earlier Ungulates and the modern pigs have however well-developed tusks as well as the full number of front teeth.

Artiodactyla or Even-toed Ungulates.

Ungulates are divided into four Orders in accordance with certain common structural characters which the members of each of these groups exhibit. Three of these Orders are represented in the Indian Empire. The first comprises the *Artiodactyla* or even-toed Ungulates, Indian representatives of which are oxen, sheep, goat, antelope, deer and pig. These animals differ from other Ungulates in a number of characters. The most important is the arrangement of the toes. It has been indicated that the feet of the majority of Ungulates show a reduction in the number of toes and that this reduction has been effected in different ways. The Artiodactyla always possess either two or four toes, hence their name even-toed. In all of them the first toe is absent. The second and fifth toes are either wanting or reduced in size. They form the 'petty-toes' of cattle and pigs, which are either rudimentary, or do not touch the ground when walking. The third and fourth toes are large and equal in size. They are perfectly symmetrical. Together they support the full weight body. The centre line of the foot passes between them. The two hoofs which encase these toes present a flat surface to each other, and appear like a single large hoof cleft in two; hence the name cloven-hoofed, applied to these animals. This characteristic alone is sufficient to distinguish all the members of this group.

Artiodactyla which are extraordinarily numerous both in genera, species and individuals are divided into four main groups or sections, namely:—

(1) *Pecora*, Typical ruminants—Oxen, Sheep, Goat, Antelope, Giraffe and Deer;

(2) *Tragulina* or Chevrotain;

(3) *Tylopoda* or Camel and Llama;

(4) *Suina* or Pig, Peccaries and Hippopotamus.

PECORA.

Oxen, sheep, antelope and deer are classed as typical ruminants. They are believed to be of comparatively recent evolution. Descendants of primitive Artiodactyles mainly inhabiting the old world, they first appeared about the middle of the Tertiary Era. The centre from which they spread over the earth is apparently northern Asia. Thence they extended their territory into northern Europe on the one hand and north America on the other. Later they spread southwards to tropical countries. Ruminants are distinguished by several well-marked characters. Like all cloven-hoofed animals they have only two functional toes on each foot, but the long bones, immediately connected with these toes, are fused into a single long bone called the 'cannon bone'. The side toes are rudimentary or altogether wanting. The limbs and feet of ruminants are highly specialised both for speed and endurance. Their cloven hoofs give them a surer hold on rough and irregular ground and, as they expand when sinking and close on extrication, a firmer footing in marshy land. Their teeth are distinctive.

Ruminants, in general, have no cutting teeth in the upper jaw. Their place is taken by a soft pad. The tongue is used to draw the food into the mouth. To do this effectively its surface is covered with rough points all directed towards the throat just as in the tongue of a lion or a cat. The molar or cheek teeth have long crowns capped with crescent shaped tubercles, which with wear grind down into crescentic patterns.

The name 'ruminant' describes their well-known habit of ruminating or 'chewing the cud'.

There is considerable advantage in this habit to these bulky though timid animals. They require large quantities of a particular type of food which must be thoroughly chewed before its nutrition becomes available. Through the process of rumination large quantities of food can be eaten rapidly. The necessarily longer process of chewing it can be continued when returning from the feeding grounds or during rest, or put off till a place of safety is reached. The complex stomach of the ruminant is specially designed to assist in this process. It is divided into four separate chambers. The first and largest—the paunch, serves to contain the hastily swallowed food. Here it undergoes a softening process and is returned in small quantities to the mouth to be thoroughly chewed in that familiar slow and deliberate manner. As each mouthful is reduced to pulp it is swallowed and immediately replaced by another. The pulped food now enters the second division of the stomach—the *reticulum* or honey-comb bag, so-called because its walls resemble a honeycomb. In the honeycomb bag the food is pressed and shaped and sent up the gullet again. It then passes into the third and fourth divisions of the stomach. The actual work of digestion takes place in the last chamber.

Typical Ruminants found within Indian limits are grouped in two families:

(1) The *Bovidae* or hollow-horned Ruminants which include oxen, sheep, goat and goat-antelope, antelope and gazelle,

(2) The *Cervidae* which includes the deer.

BOVIDAE OR HOLLOW-HORNED RUMINANTS.

The horns of oxen, sheep, goat, antelope and gazelle consist of two parts—a core of bone and an outer cap of tough, true, horn. In the majority of genera both the core and its horny cover are permanent during the life time of the animal. In the deer the same core of bone is present and forms the substance of the antlers. As with the hollow-horned ruminants the horns of deer are covered with a skin pad. This covering—the velvet lasts only for a certain period and is then rubbed off by the exertions of the animal, leaving behind the bony core which is popularly termed the horn. Stags however periodically shed this bony part of the horn, a state of affairs which has no parallel among hollow-horned ruminants.

The Bovidae or hollow-horned ruminants are a very extensive family, containing all the cattle, goats, sheep and the antelopes. They are distributed throughout Europe, Asia and North America. Eleven genera are found within Indian limits. These are included in 5 sub-families: (1) *Bovinae*, Domestic and Wild Cattle; (2) *Caprinae*, Sheep and Goats; (3) *Rupicaprinae*, Serow, Goral and Takin; (4) *Tragelaphinae*, Nilghai; (5) *Antilopinae*, Antelopes and Gazelle.

Sub-Family 1. *Bovinae*: *Gaur, Banting Yak and Buffalo.*

The Bovines are as a rule large and massively built animals. The neck is short and thick, the tail always long and tufted at the tip. The muzzle broad, naked and moist.

In the Indo-Malayan region there are 4 species belonging to this group, i.e. the Gaur (*Bibos gaurus*), the Banteng (*Bibos banteng*), the Yak (*Poephagus grunniens*) and the Indian Buffalo (*Bubalus bubalis*).

THE GAUR (*BIBOS GAURUS*, H. SMITH).

The Gaur, one of the noblest animals of the Indian forest, is apparently the largest of existing Bovines. A striking character in the build of a Gaur is the muscular ridge upon its shoulders which slopes down to the middle of the back where it ends in an abrupt dip. With its huge head, the muscular ridge crowning its deep body and its sturdy limbs the Gaur is the embodiment of vigour and strength. A bull may stand 6 ft. 4 ins. at the shoulder. The average height is between 5 ft. 8 ins. and 5 ft. 10 ins. Cows are about 4 ins. shorter. Gaur appear to attain their finest development in the South Indian hill ranges and in the forests of Burma and Assam.

The horns are large and massive, considerably flattened and corrugated at the base, rounded, smooth and turning inwards at the tips. Cows have smaller and less sturdy horns. They are rounder and have a narrower sweep. In bulls, a good average horn is 27 ins., anything over 30 ins., is a fine head. The spread of the horns taken together with the girth is the real test of a good head.

The newly born Gaur is a light golden yellow which soon changes to fawn, then to light brown and so to coffee brown or reddish brown—the colour of young bulls and cows. Old bulls are jet black—their bodies almost hairless. In the dim light of the forest an old cow may be mistaken for a bull; it looks almost as black. The dark colouring of the body is set off by an ashy coloured forehead and yellowish or white stockinged feet. Though often described as pale blue, the eye of the Gaur is brown. It is true that when the light falls on it at certain angles, the eyes are a beautiful blue. This is caused by the *Tapetum lucidium*, the membrane behind the eye-ball which is of a lovely peacock blue.

Though found in low forest in the neighbourhood of hills, Gaur are essentially mountain animals. They usually live in small herds, believed to comprise single families which, in quest of pasturage or from other causes, may unite to form larger herds. They graze at dusk or in the early morning and retire during the hotter hours of the day to the seclusion of the jungle. Except when breeding, they are peaceful animals and bulls of all sizes herd in perfect amity with the cows. A young bull, when mature, generally lives away from the herd, alone or in company with other bulls. These usually keep in the vicinity of the main herd, but wander more in quest of grazing. In the mating season, the younger bulls are driven away by the master bull who obtains possession of his cows by right of conquest. The herd bull generally returns to his accustomed hermit existence till the urge to mate is on him when he will again seek the cows and dispute with other aspirants the right of lordship. Really old beasts past the urge or capacity to mate lead truly solitary lives.

Gaur are by nature timid animals usually shunning the neighbourhood of man. They have a keen scent but comparatively poor eyesight and hearing.

Gaur range through the larger hill forests of India, Burma and the Malay Peninsula. The eastern limits of their territory is imperfectly known. The Gaur of the Malay forests is regarded as a distinct race. It is distinguished from Gaur inhabiting the Indian Peninsula by the shape of its forehead which is less concave, the great arch of bone between the horns being less prominent or practically absent.

The Gyal or Mythun (*Bibos frontalis*) is the product of interbreeding between a bull Gaur and domestic cattle. At the fourth generation the true stage of mythun is reached—an animal of lesser stature than the Gaur, shorter limbs and usually a well developed dewlap. The arched ridge between the horns and the concave forehead of the Gaur disappear. In the Mythun the vertex of the skull between the horns is straightened and the forehead flat. The horns show a slight upward curve without the terminal inward sweep. If breeding with domestic cattle is continued, the high dorsal crest is reduced to a mere hairy thickening on the back, the horns become more cow-like and the domestic cows' varied colouring begins to appear. Mythun are found in the mountainous tracts from North Cachar; through Manipur, to the Lushai and Chin Hills. They are the peculiar and characteristic possession of the hill tribes inhabiting this region.

THE BANTING OR TSAINE (*BIBOS BANTENG BIRMANICUS* LYD.).

The Banting, the Wild Ox of Burma, is a smaller animal than the Gaur, nevertheless he is massively built and stands quite 5 ft. 6 ins. at the shoulder or even higher. He is longer in the leg and the dorsal ridge is less prominent but he has the same sturdiness of limb and displays the same agility and vigour of movement as his relative.

The high concave forehead and 'roman' nose of the Gaur is wanting in the Banting. The horns are connected by a hairless mass of horny substance as hard as the skull beneath. The horns grow differently. They stand out at right angles to the skull and then turn upwards and inwards somewhat abruptly. They have the same rugged corrugations in front as in the horns of a Gaur, but are less massive. The colouring is perhaps lighter. Good average horns measure about 24 ins. in length with a girth of 14 ins. and a spread of 25 to 30 ins. Anything over 25 may be regarded as a good head. Young bulls and cows have cylindrical horns, those of cows grow almost straight upwards, are smooth throughout with but little girth.

Cows and young bulls are a bright chestnut with a white face, white stockings and a distinctive white patch on the buttocks. Young bulls sometimes show white spots on the flanks which in time merge and turn a dirty grey. Older animals are described as being yellowish brown, sometimes turning into a soiled grey on the sides. Old bulls usually have the face down to the muzzle dirty white, almost approaching grey. The coat may be entirely grey or khaki, sometimes dark chocolate brown, more rarely, quite black like the Javanese Banting. Ordinarily, in Burma, the older the bull the lighter in colour it becomes. Burmese domestic cattle tend to resemble Banting, in colour they have white patches on the buttocks and white stockings. Banting occasionally consort with domestic cattle.

The Banting, unlike the Gaur, prefers flat or undulating country. In hill country they do not ascend to great elevations and keep to the lower slopes. During the early rains they enter bamboo jungles to browse on the young shoots and during the hot weather may seek the shade of heavy jungle and cane brakes. In general they prefer lighter kinds of forests. They wander about visiting different grounds at different seasons of the year, their migrations being influenced by the pasturage.

The herding and mating habits of the Banting are in no way different to the Gaur. Master bulls take possession of the cows during the mating season and otherwise lead a solitary existence.

The Banting is a shyer and much warier animal than the Gaur, the sense of scent, sight and hearing are acutely developed.

The range of the Banting includes Burma, Siam, the Malay Peninsula, Borneo and Java. About 5 races have been described within this area.

THE YAK (*POEPHAGUS GRUNNIENS*).

An adult bull Yak stands about 5 ft. 6 ins. at the shoulder and may reach over 6 ft. It is a massively built animal with a drooping head, high humped shoulders a straight back, and short sturdy limbs.

Shaggy fringes of coarse hair hang from its flanks, cover chest, shoulders, thighs, the lower half of the tail and form a bushy tuft between its horns and a great mane upon its neck. Its great bulk, wild unkempt appearance and glaring eyes give the Yak a formidable aspect. Conspicuous and distinctive as is this clothing of long hairs, the Yak receives additional warmth through the rigorous winters from a dense under-coat of soft closely matted hair. In the spring the under fur is shed; it comes away in great masses and, though completely separated from the skin, adheres in untidy scattered patches to his hairy body. A baby Yak differs markedly from its parents in the absence of the long hair fringes, which are not noticeable in the calves until the second or third month.

The horns of a Yak are more or less rounded and quite smooth. In old bulls, the horns may be slightly compressed at the base but are never flat or corrugated as in the Gaur or Banting.

The colour of a wild Yak is a uniform blackish brown with a little white about the muzzle. Domestic Yaks of mixed breed frequently display a tendency to piebald colouring.

An inhabitant of the coldest, wildest and most desolate mountains of the Tibetan Plateau, where both arctic and desert conditions prevail, the Yak lives in a continuous struggle with the fiercest elements of Nature.

They are seldom found in very large herds, except in the spring when the cows and calves congregate on the grazing grounds. Bulls are generally solitary or found in small parties of three or four, except in the rutting season in late autumn and winter when the master bull is usually accompanied by 4 or 5 cows. Wild Yak cross freely with Ladaki cattle.

Yak feed in the mornings and evenings on the wiry grasses which grow in the valleys and have been noticed eating quantities of salt earth which in some parts cover the ground with a white crust. They retire to the steep barren hillsides to rest and ascend to great elevations.

Yak display an amazing agility in climbing; a herd is said to travel in single file, each member carefully placing its feet in the imprints left by the hoofs of the one preceding it.

The Yak is restricted to Tibet and the adjacent districts of China.

THE INDIAN WILD BUFFALO OR ARNA (*BUBALUS BUBALIS*, L.)

Wild Buffaloes are much larger than the tame buffalo and generally more hairy. A bull from the Godaveri district scaled 2,001 lbs. A large bull stands 5 ft. 6 ins. at the shoulder and may even reach 6 ft. Though it has a finer carriage, the Wild Buffalo differs little from the tame. Domestication has scarcely changed it.

There are said to be two varieties of Indian Wild Buffalo—one with straight horns turned up at the tips; the other with horns which curve upwards to form a semicircle. Both types may be found together in the same herd and there is much inter-grading between the two forms. The horns are flat and triangular in section; those of cows are less massive and vary less in shape. Occasionally, a cow with a fine length of horn is seen. The largest known horn—a cow's—is 77 3/8 ins. in length. Giants of this size must be exceptional.

Like the tame, the Wild Buffalo is a slaty black animal. The legs are a dirty white beginning just above hock and the knee—in this they resemble Gaur. The new born calf is light coloured—almost yellow. Some domestic buffaloes have the same white legs and some show a white patch between the horns.

Wild Buffaloes move about in small herds. In their social life they follow the custom of their tribe. During the rut, the younger bulls are temporarily driven out, the master bull taking possession of the cows.

The younger bulls or a solitary old bull, powerless to obtain lordship over a herd, frequently mix and breed with tame buffaloes which are driven into the forests to graze.

The rut is said to commence at the end of the rains and the young are born mainly between March and May.

Wild Buffaloes live almost entirely upon grass. Grass lands—not always marsh—interspersed with nullahs provide the conditions they prefer. They have no fear of approaching villages, come to village tanks to drink and, during the rains, frequently enter cultivation.

In India, the Wild Buffalo is found in the grass jungles of the Terai, in the plains of the Ganges and Brahmaputra in Assam, in Midnapore and Orissa and in the south-eastern portion of the Central Provinces. The numerous herds of Wild Buffalo, once seen in the C. P., are now a mere tradition. Association with domestic cattle places the Wild Buffaloes in constant danger to disease to which it is very susceptible. This is one of the animals which requires strict protection if it is not to be exterminated. An allied race of our Wild Buffalo occurs in Borneo—it is smaller in build and carries smaller horns.

ii. Sub-Family II.: *Caprinae.*

Sheep and Goats.

Sheep and Goats form the second division of Bovines. The majority of species inhabit the Highlands of Central Asia. This is in marked contrast to Africa where only 3 members of the group are present and these restricted to the northern parts of the Continent. Three species of wild sheep and three species of wild goats are found within our frontiers. They inhabit the Himalayas and the trans-Himalayan countries, the hill ranges of the Punjab, Sind and Baluchistan. The Himalayan and the Nilgiri Thar are also included in the present group.

Sheep differ in some ways from Goats. Their horns curl forwards by the sides of the face or outwards in an open spiral. The horns of Goats are situated close together, immediately above the eyes and spring upwards in the same plane as the forehead. They are either spirally twisted or scimitar shaped. Sheep usually have shorter tails, the males do not grow a beard nor have they the strong unpleasant odour of goats.

Most sheep have a small gland below the eye which lies in a corresponding depression in the skull and a small gland in each foot between the hoofs. Goats have no face glands, no gland in the hind feet and in some cases none in the fore feet. The purpose of these foot glands in Ungulates appears to be the lubrication or greasing of the hoofs and the prevention of injury from friction. Domestic goats have glands in the fore but not in the hind feet. A hind quarter of a goat with hoofs attached therefore can be at once distinguished from a sheep's by the absence of the hollow feet-pits—a point of some domestic interest when an attempt is made to substitute goat's mutton for sheep's.

Some wild goats, like the Himalayan Ibex, are hunted for their dense soft under-fur. It is used as lining for shawls, for stockings and gloves and is woven into fine cloth called *tasi*. No wool is so rich, so soft and so full. The hair is manufactured into coarse blanketing for tents and twisted into ropes. The skin of the Himalayan Ibex, when tanned, provides the best leather for the sock-like boot worn in Kashmir and the Pamirs.

THE SHAPU OR URIAL (*OVIS VIGNEI* BLYTH).

The Wild Sheep known as the *Shapu* in Ladak, the *Oorial* in the Punjab and the *Gad* in Baluchistan lives under widely differing conditions, in its extensive range. Three geographical races are distinguished by colour and size and the form of the horns. They are the Ladak Oorial (*Ovis vignei vignei*), the Afghan Oorial (*Ovis vignei cycloceros*) and the Punjab Oorial (*Ovis vignei punjabiensis*).

The Ladak Urial stands about 3 ft. or more at the shoulder. In summer its coat is rufous grey or fawn, in winter a mixture of grey and brown. The Punjab Urial is smaller and redder in colouring. The adult Urial ram wears a great black or grizzled ruff growing from either side of the chin and meeting and extending down his throat. In older rams the ruff is grey or white in front passing into black behind. In its sleeker summer coat much of the ruff is shed. It is best developed in the Punjab race. The horns are strongly wrinkled. They are set close together and curve round in a circular sweep. In the Ladak Urial the horns usually turn inwards at the tips, in the Afghan race they tend to turn outwards and form an open spiral, in the Salt Range, Punjab, they tend to form a circle. But there is much variation in horn curvature, these divergent types may be seen in the same herd, within the same area. The record horns of the three races are as follows:—Ladak Urial 39 ins.; Afghan 41½ ins.; Punjab 38¼ ins.

In Ladak, this sheep inhabits open valleys and hill sides; in Astor, the grassy mountain slopes at moderate elevations below forest. Its environment in the Punjab is rocky scrub covered hills, in Sind and Baluchistan it is found in the barren stony ranges.

Urial are sturdy active sheep ever wary and alert. As with most wild sheep, the older rams live apart from the ewes, except during the breeding season. In the Punjab hills, the rut occurs between October and November, and the lambs are born 5½ months later, in April and early in May. In Astor, lambing takes place in June. Urial cross freely with domestic sheep.

The Ladak Urial ranges from Astor to the Zaskhar range in Ladak and probably eastwards into Tibet. The Punjab race is found from Jhelum Salt Range northwards; the Afghan race is from Baluchistan and Afghanistan and is said to include the Urial inhabiting the Khirthar range and its lower spurs in Sind.

THE NYAN OR GREAT TIBETAN SHEEP (*OVIS AMMON HODGSONI* BLYTH).

The Argali (*Ovis ammon*), the largest of all wild sheep, inhabits the Himalayas and the highlands of Central Asia. Over this extensive region this sheep varies in different areas in the form of its horns, colouring or size. Several more or less distinctive races are recognised. Two races of the Argali—the Nyan or Great Tibetan Sheep (*Ovis ammon hodgsoni*) and Marcopolo's Sheep (*Ovis ammon poli*) occur within our frontiers.

The Great Tibetan Sheep stands from 3½ to 4 ft. at the shoulder. Long in the leg, graceful and light—it suggests an antelope in build. Its massive wrinkled horns, 16 to 19 ins. in girth, curve in almost complete circle. The record, a picked-up head, measures 57 ins.

The ram is light brown with darker withers. His throat, rump, underparts and limbs are white. Adult rams have white heads and develop a white ruff about the neck much of which is shed with the winter coat.

The Tibetan Plateau, where Nyan live, presents a wilderness of desolate plains and low undulating sand hills, scorched in summer and swept by icy winds through the freezing winters. In this desert terrain the sheep are naturally migratory and wander to wherever food and water is to be got. In the spring, when the melting snows cause the scanty herbage to sprout, they frequent the borders of the snow line or enter the ravines, some of which hold trickling streams whose banks are covered with low bushes and herbage. They summer in the higher levels above 15,000 ft. and in winter descend to the shelter of the lower valleys. They feed early in the morning and again in the evening and climb some bare hillside to rest during the day. They avoid the damp snow and select some dry spot on the stony slope, kicking out with their feet a shallow 'form' in which to lie down. Their colouration is highly protective. It is difficult to discover them except in movement. When lying down they usually keep their heads erect but, when sleeping, lie with outstretched necks, the big rams resting their great curling horns on the ground.

In the spring, the sexes separate. Through the summer the older rams herd together in small parties and usually live apart from the ewes and yearlings. They rejoin them in the late autumn when the mating season begins. The young are born in May and early June, when the ewes seek the shelter of the more secluded valleys to lamb. This sheep was once plentiful in the country to the eastward of Chang-Chemo in Ladak and across the Tibetan border in the region lying to the north-east of the Pangkong Lake. They occasionally cross into Spiti, Nepal and Kumaon and are also found in the neighbourhood of the Tso Lhama Lake in the extreme north of Sikkim.

MARCOPOLO'S SHEEP (*OVIS AMMON POLI* BLYTH).

Marcopolo's Sheep is a race of the Argali. It has less massive horns which form an open and extended spiral.

An adult ram is from 11 to 12 hands high at the shoulder and scales about 250 lbs. Like the Nyan, he is long legged and light in build. His magnificent horns, deeply wrinkled and the colour of old ivory, curve in a circle, then extend outwards in a bold sweep. The record pair is 75 ins. in length. The average length is about 52 ins. with a girth of 15 ins. at the base. In winter the adult ram has a creamy white head, legs and belly. His flanks are grey, merging into the darker brown of the back. The general colouring is that of the bare boulder strewn terrain in which this sheep lives. The colour makes the animal almost invisible, except in movement. Young lambs are uniform dark grey; yearlings a lighter mouse grey. The heavy winter coat is replaced about the end of May by the short paler summer pelage.

Rolling boulder strewn plateaux, cut up by broad stony nullahs, set against a sky line of snow-capped mountains—this is the dead and desert region in which *Ovis poli* live. In the spring the little patches of grass along the snow line and the nullahs, where a small lake or winding stream produces herbage, form their habitual resorts. Their food is then limited to the bunches of wiry grass and later to a species of wild onion which springs up in the sandy tracts. After a hard winter, conditions are most arduous and many die of starvation. In the summer, when there is a fair growth of grass over the Pamirs, the veteran males ascend into the higher and more remote nullahs. They feed morning and evening and go up some bare hillside to rest during the day; always moving in single file, the big ones leading. Excellent of sight and wonderfully keen in scent, when alarmed, they stand stock still or crowd together stamping the ground with their forefeet, even advancing nearer. All at once one bounds away, the herd follows heads held high, galloping with long easy strides but, intensely curious, they go a short distance, then turn and stop to see what disturbed them.

In their breeding habits differ in no way from the Tibetan Nyan. The rams fight as sheep do—a frontal attack with lowered head, the horns meeting in a clash which can be heard a long way off, or they charge alongside to strike sideways at the ribs and flanks.

Within Indian limits, *Ovis poli* are found only in Hunza. The Mir of Hunza has given them for some years strict protection in his territory. They exist in more or less reduced numbers in most of the side valleys of the Tagdumbash Pamirs. In the Russian Pamirs they still seem to be plentiful.

BHARAL (*PSEUDOIS NAHOOR* HODGSON).

In structure and habits the Bharal holds a place intermediate between the sheep and goats. Its horns are rounded and smooth, and curve backwards over the neck. This sheep has no face glands. Their position is however marked by a small bare patch of skin. In these characters the Bharal approaches the goats. But a Bharal ram is not bearded nor has he the unpleasant 'goaty' odour. Again, Bharal may have glands between the hoofs in all four feet; in goats these are always absent in the hind limbs.

A Bharal ram is about 3 ft. at the shoulder, stout and powerfully built. It scales, according to the time of the year, from 120 to 150 lbs. Its coat is dense. The general colour of the head and upper parts is brownish grey, suffused with slaty blue, browner in summer and more distinctly slaty grey in winter. The colour in any season blends perfectly with the blue shale and rock of the open hillsides where Bharal live. The face and chest in old rams is black. A black stripe runs along the middle of each flank and down the front of the legs. All these black markings are absent in ewes. The horns are smooth and marked with fine striations—lines of growth. They curve outwards and downwards and, in well grown rams, curl backwards at the tips. The record head from near Gyantse, Tibet, is 33¼ ins.; 23 ins. may be described as a good head.

To find Bharal one must seek the higher altitudes, neighbouring on 16,000 ft. in summer, and rarely below 12,000 in the winter. In the main Himalayan Range they are found on the levels between the tree and snow line where there is rich and abundant grass. In the Zaskar and Ladak ranges the slopes above tree line are bare and they find their food in the occasional patches of coarse grass, moss and dwarf shrubs. Bharal climb like goats and take to the most difficult and inaccessible places when disturbed but never enter forest or scrub. They live in large flocks, numbering as many as 200. These mixed flocks of rams and ewes may contain well grown males but the mature rams keep somewhat to themselves. In spring and summer the really old rams seek the higher levels and rejoin the females and younger males in September.

Unlike the Urial the Bharal will not cross with tame sheep nor is it as easy to tame.

Though typically a Tibetan animal, the Bharal is also found in Sikkim, Ladak and Nepal.

THE ASIATIC IBEX (*CAPRA SIBRICA* MEY.).

The Genus Capra (Goats) is represented in our area by three species:—The Asiatic Ibex (*Capra sibrica*), the Sind Wild Goat (*Capra hircus blythi*) and the Markhor (*Capra falconeri*).

There are various geographical races of the Asiatic Ibex—a species closely related to the Alpine Ibex (*Capra ibex*) of the Swiss Alps. The Asiatic animal is considerably larger in size; standing as high as 42 inches at the shoulder. It is a sturdy, thick set goat, with a great beard and a coat of coarse brittle hairs. In winter, a dense under-fur of wool helps it to withstand the intense cold of its native mountains. The colour is variable. In general, the winter coat is yellowish white more or less tinged with brown and grey. In summer, the general hue is dark brown with irregular white patches. A male in good condition, weighs slightly over 200 lbs. The female is yellowish brown and insignificant to look at. The great scimitar shaped horns of the buck are flat and bossed with bold ridges in front. They are usually larger in the Tian Shan Race (*Capra sibrica almasyi*). The record length being 58 ins. The Kashmir Ibex is known as *Capra sibrica skyn*. It is a paler, brown-coloured animal with rather shorter horns than the Tian Shan Ibex. The record head from Gilgit is 55 ins. The various races of Asiatic Ibex, said to be distinguishable by the form of the horns, and differences in general colouring, cannot be satisfactorily separated by these characters which vary considerably in the same areas.

Ibex live in flocks numbering from a dozen to 40 or 50, though much larger herds have been seen. Their favourite grounds lie in the higher elevations well above the tree line. Here, on the precipitous sides of some cliff or nullah, patches of grass and small plants give them grazing. They feed early in the mornings and evenings and then climb up higher into the forbidding shelter of rock and snow to rest. Sentinels, usually an old ewe or ewes, are posted on some projecting rock or commanding point. Ever vigilant, they utter the shrill whistle of alarm which sends the flock dashing down and then upwards again, away to shelter among the precipitous steeps.

In spring and early summer, the old males are usually with or near the females and young but later in the summer the patriarchs retire to the more inaccessible mountains. They rejoin the main herds about October. The young are born in May and early June. The Himalayan Ibex inhabits the Western Himalayas on both sides of the main Himalayan Range and the mountain ranges which lie beyond in Kashmir and Baltistan. Its eastern limits are set by the upper reaches of the Sutlej River, east of which it does not occur.

THE SIND WILD GOAT (*CAPRA HIRCUS BLYTHI* HUME).

The Sind Wild Goat is a relative of the wild goat of the Caucasus (*Capra hircus aegagarus*). It is distinguished by its smaller size. The species is of special interest as being the chief ancestral stock from which the various breeds of domestic goats are derived. A full grown buck is from 32 to 37 inches at the shoulder—a handsome bearded goat; brownish grey in winter, close haired, yellowish or rufous brown in summer. The under parts are whitish. Old males are lighter coloured. Well grown bucks have a dark stripe running from the nape of the neck along the back to the root of the tail and a cross stripe down each shoulder. The face, the chin with its beard, the throat, the tail, front of the legs, except the knees and a stripe along the flanks are dark brown. The horns are long and scimitar like. They sweep back in a graceful curve. Unlike the flat and regularly knobbed horns of the Ibex, they are compressed in front into a narrow jagged keel. The record length is about 52 ins. Anything over 40 ins. is a good head.

The Sind Wild Goat lives in small or large herds. In the barren hills of the Khirthar range their environment is one of jagged rock and loose stones, thorn and cactus with little or no water—a furnace of heat in summer; freezing cold in winter. Like all goats they are active, agile and surefooted leaping from ledge to ledge, stopping short on the steep hillside to balance on a pinnacle of rock where there is scarce a foothold. They go to rest on some commanding ridge from whence the sentinels of the flock can obtain a view of the surrounding slopes.

The 'bezoar stone' formerly famed in Europe and regarded in the East as an antidote to poison and as remedy in many diseases is a hard concretion found in the stomach of this goat.

The Sind Wild Goat inhabits the barren hills of Baluchistan and Western Sind, but not east or north-east of the Bolan Pass and Quetta. Here it is replaced by the Markhor.

THE MARKHOR (*CAPRA FALCONERI* WAGNER).

The Markhor, the grandest of all wild goats, stands about 41 ins. high at the shoulder. An old male, with his great horns, flowing beard and his mane, falling from his neck and shoulders to his knees, has a dignified and patriarchal appearance. The long and silky haired winter coat is a rusty iron grey; in summer, the hair is shorter. It takes a reddish brown tinge. Old males become more or less white. Young bucks are equally shaggy though not as copiously bearded as the veterans. Female are dark fawn and about half the size of a well grown male. Some wear a scanty beard. Markhor carry magnificent horns. These show more or less constant variation in form in different areas. Otherwise there is nothing to really distinguish the 4 known races. The typical Markhor (*Capra falconeri falconeri*) inhabits Astor. In this area the horns diverge widely and form an open spiral. The maximum recorded length is 60 ins. Horns of this type are also seen in Baltistan and Gilgit. Markhor from the Pirpinjal and Kaj-i-nag Mountains (*Capra f. cashmiriensis*) have horns which diverge less and, in fine heads, show two complete twists or spirals. The record is 65 ins. This type is also common in Baltistan, Gilgit and Chitral. In the hills on the northern edge of Peshawar, the horns lose their imposing spiral and assume the straight corkscrew pattern, typical of Markhor living in the mountains of North Afghanistan. The race is known as Kabul Markhor (*Capra f. megaceros*). The straightening of the horns and the accentuation of the spiral twist reaches its extreme in the Suleman Markhor (*Capra f. jerdoni*), which is found in the Suleman Mountains in the Trans-Indus District of the Punjab. The Markhor of the mountain ranges of Baluchistan, curiously enough, show two forms of horns—one, resembling the wide spanned Astor type and the other the Pirpinjal form with its more modified sweep.

The character of the country through which Markhor range varies greatly. The Sulemans and the hills of the North-West Frontier are covered with thorn and scrub and exposed to terrific heat in summer. There Markhor must live under very different conditions to those whose environment is the pine forests and snow bound scarps of the mountains of Kashmir. Markhor associate in small herds usually selecting the most broken and precipitous country. They do not like snow and seldom go higher than the snow line and, in winter, descend to comparatively low levels. Their sensitiveness to cold is attributed to the absence of under-fur or *pashm* with which the Ibex is so well provided. Unlike Ibex, which keep to the rugged ravines above the tree line, the Markhor delights in rocky forest and seeks concealment as much as possible. They are sometimes in large mixed herds but in summer the veterans generally live apart, alone, or four or five males together. The rut is said to take place in December in the Himalayas and in October and November with the straight horned races.

(*To be continued*).

PRINTED AT THE DIOCESAN PRESS, MADRAS—1934. C9987.

THE HIMALAYAN TAHR (*HEMITRAGUS JEMLAHICUS.* H. SM.).

The Tahr does not compare well with his big-horned relatives the Ibex and Markhor. It is a wild goat with a finely formed head, narrow erect ears, a heavy body and long robust limbs. A well grown male stands from 36-40 in. at the shoulder and scales near 200 lbs. While the hair on the Tahr's head and face is short its body is covered with tangled masses of coarse, flowing hair. It grows longest on the neck and shoulders where it develops into a mane which sweeps down to the knees. An old buck poised on some precipitous cliff presents a grand picture. The colouring is very variable. Generally it is a deep reddish brown and there is a dark dorsal streak—not always distinct. Old males are darker, particularly about the back and quarters. Ewes and young males are lighter brown; kids much paler.

The horns are short and close set. They are stout at the base, keeled in front and wrinkled, except towards the tips. They curve backwards and in old bucks continue downwards. They are about 15 in. in length with a circumference of 10-11 in. at the base. The record measures 16½ with a girth of 10½. Females are smaller in build. Their horns are dimunitive. They are easily recognised by their lighter colouring and less shaggy coats.

Tahr live in a precipitous terrain of towering cliffs, rock and forest. Because of the difficult country they inhabit, it is said that few Himalayan game animals so tax the skill and endurance of the hunter.

About March and April before the snows have melted, Tahr crowd into the bottoms of the valleys. In summer, the older males herd together or live singly. They frequent the densest undergrowth and the most precipitous cliffs. They rejoin the females in late September or October. During the rutting season the males are always fighting and many are said to be killed by falling down the crags.

Tahr feed in grassy spots among rocks. If alarmed they go off with great speed and clatter but soon halt and turn to stare at the intruder. They generally follow the guidance of an old male and seek security in the almost perpendicular precipices. Their sense of sight and smell are both keenly developed. The range of the Tahr includes the Himalayas from Kashmir to Bhutan but does not extend to the northern side of the Vale of Kashmir. Tahr are common on the southern slopes of the Himalayas but do not occur on the Tibetan side of the range.

THE NILGIRI TAHR (*HEMITRAGUS HYLOCRIUS* BLYTH).

Frequently misnamed the Nilgiri Ibex, the Nilgiri Tahr is a near relative of the Himalayan species. It is slightly larger than the Himalayan Tahr, standing 39-42 in. at the shoulder. Its short crisp coat, the rounded outer surface of its horns and the presence of only a single pair of teats are other distinguishing characters.

The general colour of the animal is a dark yellowish brown, paler on the undersurface. Does and young bucks are grey. With age the bucks get a very deep brown—almost black coat with a distinctive light 'saddle' patch on the loins. From a distance the saddle looks almost white. In build bucks are far heavier and sotckier than the does.

The horns, almost in contact at the base, rise parallel for some length then diverge and curve downwards in a bold sweep. They are deeply wrinkled. The knotted keel in front, so distinctive in the horns of the Himalayan Tahr, is absent. The record buck horns measure 17½ with a girth of 9⅞ in. The record doe 14 in. Nilgiri heads are small in comparison to those found in the more southerly ranges.

Nilgiri Tahr live on the open cliffs and when alarmed take shelter on the precipitous slopes. They feed in flocks on the grassy downs which top the summits, grazing in the early morning or late afternoon and resting during the hot hours of the day. One or more does stand sentinel over the resting herd. While exceedingly watchful against any danger approaching from below, they are frequently outwitted by the enemy from above. Panthers levy the heaviest toll on the herds.

During the south-west monsoon Tahr generally move down to lower elevations. Old bucks desert the herds during the hot weather and, more often than not, are found solitary. Tahr sometimes have two young but one is more usual. The kids are dropped most commonly during the hot weather.

The isolated distribution of this wild goat so far south of the usual range is interesting and is taken to indicate the existence at some remote epoch of the earth's history of conditions which enabled Tahr to inhabit the country now lying between the Himalayas and the Nilgiris.

Strict preservation has saved the Tahr from extermination in the Nilgiris. From these hills its range extends to the Anamallais and thence southwards along the Western Ghats.

Sub-Family III. *Rupicaprinae*: Goat-Antelopes.

Serow, Goral and Takin.

The Goat-Antelopes are said to hold an intermediate position between the Goats and that heterogeneous assemblage of animals collectively known as 'Antelopes'. All of them are mountain animals. Most have a more or less goat-like build, goat-like teeth and short tails. Relatively small cylindrical horns are present in both sexes.

Serow, Goral and Takin belong to this group. It also includes the Chamois (*Rupicapra*), the type which gives its name to the group, and the Rocky Mountain Goat of North America.

Serow and Goral have distinctive conical horns. They curve backwards and have not the terminal hook seen in the straight horns of the Chamois. Though there is a superficial resemblance between them, Serow and Goral differ much in the structure of the skull. Further, unlike Goral, Serow have well-developed face glands which rest in a depression in the skull. The gland opens with its small orifice in front of the eye. At times the opening looks like a small sore. It exudes a whitish secretion which, when dry, has the consistency and smell of gum arabic. Serow have a strong goaty odour. As in sheep and goats it appears to come from the surface of the skin and not from any special glands.

Goral are much smaller animals than Serow. They have no face glands but are furnished with foot glands similar to those found in sheep. These glands open by a small orifice in front of the pastern, above the hoof. It is not known whether Serow have them. Strangely enough, in the structure of its skull, the Goral approaches the Takin. A kinship is here suggested which one would not easily suspect from the widely different appearance of these two animals.

The Takin is a large heavily built, aberrant form of goat-antelope. It lacks that lightness of limb and body to which Serow and Goral owe their agility. The horns, which are thick and nearly in contact at the base, grow outwards, downwards or forwards and then take an abrupt curve upwards or backwards in the same direction as the plane of the face.

THE SEROW (*CAPRICORNIS SUMATRAENSIS* POCOCK).

With its large head and donkey-like ears, its thick neck and short limbs the Serow is an ungainly creature. Its habit of standing with its forelegs astraddle, the hoofs widely splayed and the head thrust downwards adds to its awkward appearance. Both sexes are similar in build. A full grown Serow is from 36-38 in. at the shoulder and scales from 170-200 lbs.

The coat is coarse and rather thin in Serow which live at lower elevations. Its colour varies so much that it is difficult to describe. It ranges from grizzled black or blackish grey-roan to red. In the darker animals the head, neck and the mane, which covers the nape and withers, is grizzled black. The black passes into rusty red on the shoulders, flanks and lower thighs and turns a dirty grey on the inside of the limbs and belly. There is a varying amount of white on the muzzle, throat and chest. In the Chin Hills and Arakan a red race of Serow (*C. s. rubidus*) occurs. In the Himalayan races the limbs are chestnut above and dirty white below from this there is a transition to the Malay serows in which the limbs are wholly black.

Horns are common to both sexes. They are black, conical and closely wrinkled for three quarters of their length. They run to 10 or 11 in.

In the Himalayas the Serow favours an elevation between 6,000 to 10,000 ft. In the Burmese hill ranges they may be met with at a height which varies from 700 to 8,000 ft.

Serow live in the recesses of thickly wooded gorges whose boulder strewn slopes and shallow caves give them shelter from the weather. In the mornings and evenings they come out to feed on the rank herbage of the more open slopes. They are more or less solitary creatures though four or five may be seen feeding on the same hill. Their movements belie their awkward appearance. They are exceedingly active animals, not only on rock but also on flat ground. When disturbed, serow dash away with a hissing snort. Their call is a whistling scream. The female usually has one kid at birth, sometimes two. In the Himalayas the rut commences at the end of October and the young are born in May and June. In Burma the young are born about the end of September. The period of gestation is said to be about 7 months.

Serow range from the Himalayas to the mountains of China and southwards through Burma and the Malay countries. They are also found in Formosa and Japan. Eight races have been described from British India and the Strait Settlements all localised forms of a single variable species.

GORAL (*NEMORHAEDUS*).

Three species of Goral are found within the Indian Empire:—The Grey Himalayan Goral (*Nemorhaedus goral* Hardwicke) of Kashmir and the Western Himalayas, the Brown Goral (*N. hodgsoni* Pocock) of Nepal and Sikhim, and the Burmese Goral (*N. griseus* Milne-Edwards) found in Burma, Eastern Tibet and Southern China.

The Goral is sometimes called the Himalayan Chamois. It has little in common with the Chamois and is distinct in the form of its horns, and the colouring and shagginess of its coat. Its kinship with the Takin has already been suggested. The Goral is a goat-like animal standing about 26-28 in. at the shoulder.

The general colour of the Grey Goral is a yellowish grey suffused with black. Individuals differ, but no Grey Goral has the pale area of the hairs tinged with rufous or brown. The chin, upper lip, underside of the jaws and throat patch are white. The dark spinal stripe if present, does not pass beyond the withers. There is no stripe down the middle of the tail and none up the back of the thighs. The Brown Goral is distinguished by its golden or rufous brown coat, speckled with black. The black spinal stripe reaches to the root of the tail but tapers away and is indistinct on the croup. The tail is black above. A dark ill-defined stripe runs up the back of the thigh from the hocks.

The Goral of Burma is distinguishable from the two Himalayan forms by two main characters. The tail is larger; about 5 ins. long in the adult. The black stripe on the fore-leg does not pass over the knee as in the Himalayan Gorals but turns aside and runs down the outer side of the cannon bone on to the back of the fetlock.

Goral have short insignificant horns. They diverge slightly, curve backwards and are marked with rings or ridges for the greater part of their length. The record pair of Grey Goral horns measures 8⅞ in.

Goral frequent hillsides or rocky forest clad ground. They graze in small parties of 4-8 individuals. Old bucks are frequently solitary. In the Himalayas, Goral favour an elevation of 3,000-9,000 ft. though they may ascend to and have been observed at 13,000-14,000 ft. In the Arakan and Chin Hills, Goral are found above 3,000 ft. In Garhwal new born young have been observed in April,

TAKIN (*BUDORCAS TAXICOLOR* HODGS.).

There are said to be three species of Takin:—The Mishmi Takin (*Budorcas taxicolor* Hodgs.), the Tibetan Takin (*B. tibetana* M.-Eds.) and Bedford's Takin (*B. bedfordi* Thomas). So far as is known the Mishmi Takin occurs in Bhutan Himalaya in the Mishmi Hills, on the Burma Assam Tibet frontier and in the Mountains of the Salween Irrawady divide. The Tibetan Takin is found in Eastern Tibet and Western Sze Chuan. Bedford's Takin in the Tsinling Range in Shensi, W. China. It is possible that the three forms are geographical races of a single species.

The Bhutan Takin is recognised as a separate race, *B. t. whitei*, because of its smaller size, darker colouring and smaller saddle.

The Takin is a clumsy heavy animal which from the shape of its horns looks as if it might have some relation to the gnu or musk ox, though there is no structural affinity between them. Its most striking feature is its immense convex 'face', heavy mouth and tremendously thick neck. The muzzle, except for a bare spot at the extremity is covered with hair. It is a character seen also in the yak and is probably associated with life at high altitudes, where the snow in winter has to be scraped away to get at the vegetation beneath. The Takin's heavy body is supported by exceptionally short, thick legs, thicker than those of a bison. Its withers are slightly raised and its narrow back arches in the centre and slopes downward to the root of the tail.

There is great variety of colour in Takin, ranging from dark brown to golden yellow. The withers are conspicuously lighter in tone. Adult males of the Mishmi Takin are golden yellow merging into dark brown or black on the flanks and quarters. There is a dark dorsal stripe. Young males are reddish brown in front merging into black. Calves all black. Females are greyer than the bulls with no trace of yellow. The dark dorsal stripe is inconspicuous in females and young males.

The horns of a young Takin grow straight up from the head with an outward tendency. Later they grow outwards and downwards. In the final stage the horns grow forwards, bend downwards and outwards with the points growing up.

Takin live in the steepest and most thickly wooded declivities of their native mountains. In the Mishmi hills they have been seen in tropical forest as low as 3,000-4,000 ft. They are usually found in dense bamboo and rhododendron jungle at an elevation of 7,000-10,000 ft. In the summer months they collect in herds of considerable size as many as 300 have been observed congregated about a hot spring to drink. They went to cover at mid-day and came out in the late afternoon. In the winter the herds are said to break up into smaller parties. In Western China the rut takes place in July, August. The calves, usually one at birth are dropped towards the end of March or early in April.

Sub-Family IV. *Antilopinae*: ANTELOPES.

The Antelopes form an extensive group of ruminating ungulates which includes almost all the remaining members of the Bovine family. Although the term 'antelope' is in common use and though most antelopes are easily recognised, they are so numerous, so diverse in form that it is difficult to distinguish them as a whole from the oxen on the one hand and the goats on the other. They represent a transition between the two. Antelopes are the most generalised and oldest known representatives of the *Bovidae*. It is believed that the more distinctive and more specialised members of the family which we have so far described have been derived from them. In general, antelopes are light and graceful in build. Fleet of foot, they depend for their safety on great speed. Horns may or may not be present in both sexes. The bony core of an antelope's horn is nearly solid throughout and not honeycombed as are the horns of oxen. In the structure of their teeth some Antelopes resemble oxen, others, the sheep and goats.

Antelopes very generally have a gland beneath the eye, which distinguishes them from oxen and goats. The prominent glands below the eyes of the Indian Antelope or Black Buck attract the attention of most people. When closed the gland takes the form of a vertical slit of black, nearly hairless skin. This opens into a deep hair lined and perforated pocket into which the secretion of the underlying gland exudes.

It is difficult to surmise the exact function of these glands. They are present, as we have already seen, in other ruminants. They may have a sexual significance. They are particularly active in certain seasons and generally better developed in males than in females. But apart from this they may also serve as scent glands and, like the foot and other skin glands serve as a guide in keeping individuals of a herd together.

Antelopes are not nearly so well represented in India and Malaya as they are in Africa. If we exclude the widely spread group of gazelles the only Antelopes found outside Africa, Syria or Arabia are the Black Buck which is confined to India, the Saiga Antelope of Tartary and the Chiru of Tibet.

THE CHIRU OR TIBETAN ANTELOPE (*PANTHALOPS HODGSONI* ABEL.).

In the elevated and barren plateaux of Tibet there is a species of antelope which is remarkable for its curiously swollen snout and long, elegant horns. This is the Chiru, an antelope which is said to be the living prototype of the fabulous unicorn. Its long and slender horns, if seen in profile, may well suggest a unicorned animal. The Chiru is classed in a separate sub-family of antelopes—the *Panthalopinac* of which it is the only representative. The nearest relatives of the Chiru are the Saiga Antelope of Eastern Russia and the Impala of Africa. The Saiga carries to greater degree the curious snout development of Chiru. Its nose is inflated and prolonged into a downwardly bent, trunk-like proboscis. This inflation of the nose may have some connection with the high altitudes in which these animals live. At the side of each nostril, the Chiru has a large lateral chamber or sac whose function may assist breathing in the rarefied atmosphere of its native wilds.

Another peculiarity of the Chiru is the unusual development of the inguinal or groin glands. Perhaps the function of these glands, which are possessed also by other ruminants, is to scent the ground and so indicate to other individuals of a herd the place where one of them has rested. Chiru are known to lie up concealed in shallow pits which they scrape out for themselves in the sand. Large scent glands are also present between the fore and hind hoofs of the Chiru. It has no face glands.

The Chiru stands about 31-32 in. at the shoulder. Its body is covered with dense wool. The colour is variable. Generally it is pale fawn above and white below. The whole of the face and a stripe down the front of each leg is black or dark brown in the bucks. The horns of the bucks rise close together; they diverge towards the tips and curve slightly forward. They reach from 24-26 in. The record pair is $27\frac{3}{4}$ in. Females are hornless.

Chiru live in the open rolling plains and the broad river valleys of the Tibetan Plateau, some 12,000-18,000 ft. above sea level. They may collect in large herds but it is more usual to find them in small parties of 3 or 4. They graze on the grass and small plants which grow on the open wind swept river flats. In summer the bucks live apart. The young are born in May and June. One young is produced at birth.

The Chiru is found only on the Tibetan Plateau. Its range extends north from the Chang-chenmo district of Ladak along the Nepal Tibetan frontier to the north of Tibet.

The Indian Bison or Gaur (Bibos gaurus, H. Smith).

The Black Buck (*Antilope cervicapra, L.*).
(*Height at shoulder 32 in.*).

The Indian Gazelle or Chinkara *(Gazella bennetti Sykes)*.
(Height at shoulder 26 in.).

The Four-horned Antelope (*Tetraceros quadricornis, Blainv.*).

The Nilgai or Blue Bull (*Boselaphus tragocamelus, Pallas*).
(*Height at shoulder 56 in.*).

The Musk-Deer (*Moschus moschiferus L.*).

The Muntjac or Barking Deer (*Muntiacus muntjak Zimm.*).
(*Height at shoulder 20-30 in.*).

The Chital or Spotted Deer *(Axis axis Erxl.)*
(Height at shoulder 36 in.).

The Hog-Deer (Hyelaphus porcinus Zimm.).
(Height at shoulder 27-29 in.).

The Sāmbar *(Rusa unicolor Kerr.)*.
(Height at shoulder 5 ft.).

The Swamp Deer *(Rucervus duvaucelli Cuv.)*.
(Height at shoulder 54 in.).

The Indian Chevrotain or Mouse Deer (*Moschiola meminna Erxl.*)

SNOW LEOPARDS.

The Leopard Cat *(Prionailurus bengalensis, Kerr.)*

The Clouded Leopard *(Neofelis nebulosa, Griffith.)*

The Stripe-necked Mungoose (Herpestes vitticollis, Bennett).

THE BLACK BUCK OR INDIAN ANTELOPE (*ANTILOPE CERVICAPRA* LINN.).

The Black Buck is the sole representative of the genus *Antilope*.

Its striking colour, its beautiful spiraled horns, which may reach the shoulder height of the animal, give it an elegance hardly equalled by any antelope. This exclusively Indian animal is perhaps the most beautiful of all its tribe.

A well-grown buck stands about 30 in. at the shoulder and on the average weighs some 80 lbs. When young, its coat, like that of the does, is a yellowish fawn. When 3 years old it commences to turn black. This darkening of the coat varies in intensity. In South India the adult buck is rarely black, his coat remains a dark brown. Well matured brown bucks may again be seen in all parts of the country. In general there is a fading in the richness of tone during the hot weather and an increase in its velvety lustre after the rains.

In the yearling buck the horns are without a spiral. In the second year a large open spiral is developed. It is believed that the full number of spiral twists are attained with the dark coat about the end of the third year. The best heads come from the dry and arid districts of the Punjab and Rajputana, the poorest from South India and the humid plains lying west of the United Provinces. Here a head above 18 in. is considered good. The record 31⅞ in. is from Jind State.

Black Buck are usually seen in herds of 20 or 30, though in Rajputana and the Punjab herds may number several hundreds. Black Buck live in open plains covered with scrub or cultivation. They feed on grass or various cereal crops. Usually Black Buck graze till mid-day and again in the late afternoon. Their sense of hearing is moderate: scent fair. Keen eye-sight and speed are their protection. When alarmed the herd moves off in a series of astonishing leaps and bounds and then breaks into a gallop. The leadership of the herd is usually vested in an old and vigilant female. There is generally an old buck in attendance who keeps in the vicinity. He frequently deserts the herd for a period taking a favoured doe with him. Black Buck breed at all seasons but mainly about February and March. Then the bucks grunt and strut about with their peculiar gait, their heads thrown well back. Their great face glands are everted and give off their strong smelling secretion. One or two fawns are born at a time, these are usually concealed by the mother in tall grass or among bushes.

Black Buck may be found practically all over the Indian plains except on the Malabar Coast. They avoid forest or hill tracts.

THE CHINKARA OR INDIAN GAZELLE (*GAZELLA BENNETTI*, SYKES.).

Three species of Gazelles inhabit the Indian Region:—The Indian Gazelle (*Gazella bennetti* Sykes), The Tibetan or Goa Gazelle (*G. picticauda* Hodgs.) and The Seistan Gazelle (*G. seistanica* Lyd.).

The Chinkara or Indian Gazelle is found practically all over the plains districts of India. It lives in small herds of 10 or 20 in waste lands broken up by nullahs and ravines, in scattered bush and thin jungle. It is common in the sandhills of the desert zone. In the Salt Range, Punjab, Chinkara have been seen as high as 4,000 ft. They do not enter forest; prefer broken country and live less in open level plains than Black Buck.

A buck Chinkara is 26 in. high at the shoulder and scales about 50 lbs. The horns which usually have 15 or 16 rings average from 10-12 in. They rarely exceed this length in Central or South India. The best heads come from the dry desert tracts of Rajputana and the North-West. The record is slightly over 16 in. Both sexes are usually horned. Though hornless females are not uncommon. The horns of the doe are smooth conical spikes usually about 4-5 in. long, slightly curved at the tip or straight and distinctly ringed at the base. Chinkara are less diurnal than Black Buck. They lie up earlier in the day and come out later in the evening. A Chinkara is a wary animal when feeding, always on the alert, always raising its head to look round. When alarmed the herd goes off at a wild pace and then stops at about 200 or 300 yds. on some eminence to turn and discover the cause of their alarm. Their food consists of grass, leaves, various crops and fruits such as gourds and melons. They go without water for long periods but will drink when they can get access to it. There is no regular breeding season. One or two fawns are born at a time.

The Tibetan Gazelle inhabits North-Eastern Ladak, the Tibetan Plateau and Shensi. It is a small gazelle, from 24-25 in. at the withers. Its slender close ringed horns rise vertically and curve sharply backwards. A good head tapes 12 in. The record is 15½ in. The summer coat is short and slate grey. In winter it is dense and pale fawn. The Seistan Gazelle, described from Siestan in Persia, is found in Baluchistan. The females are hornless. The horns of the bucks bend backwards and have their tips more or less distinctly in-turned. The greyish forehead of the older buck and the white muzzle and a whitish band at the base of the horns are distinctive.

Sub-Family V. *Tragelaphinae*: TRAGELAPHINE ANTELOPES.

The Tragelaphine Antelopes form a fifth division of the Hollow-horned Ruminants. The group is more African than Indian. It includes the African Bushbucks, Kudus, Bongo and Elands. Only two forms are found in India:—the Nilgai and the Four-horned Antelope. Tragelaphine Antelopes are characterised by the general absence of horns in the females (except in two African genera). The horns of the males are not ringed; they are keeled in front and in most genera, such as Eland, Kudu etc., they are spirally twisted. The Indian genera are characterised by the shortness and straightness of their horns, the absence of distinctive body stripes and by the possession of face glands. The hoofs are not deeply cleft as in true antelopes and there are no foot glands. The structure of the foot is practically the same as in Bovines—the molar teeth again are semi-Bovine. Lateral or false hoofs are well developed in both limbs. The muzzle is naked and the tail long.

The distributional area includes Ethiopian Africa and Peninsular India. There is reason to believe that a Tragelaphine Antelope probably existed in the Euphrates Valley during the Assyrian period.

THE FOUR-HORNED ANTELOPE (*TETRACEROS QUADRICORNIS* BLAINV.).

The Four-horned Antelope or *Chousingha* is the only Antelope with 2 pairs of horns. Of these the front pair are always the shorter. At times they are no more than horn-covered studs or mere bony knobs under the skin. The maximum length of the back pair is 4½ in., of the front 2½ in.

One of the most interesting features in this Antelope is the presence of a pair of well-developed glands between the false hoofs of the hind legs in both males and females. This is the only antelope which has such glands.

The *Chousingha* is about 25 in. high and scales near 50 lbs.

Its coarse coat is dull red brown above and white below. It lives in undulating or hill country and shelters in tall grass or open jungle—a terrain more usual to deer than to antelope. In this environment it has developed some of the habits of deer. It has a low whistling call, which the bucks repeat frequently in the hot weather and a sharp alarm note which the doe uses to guide her fawns through cover when in flight.

These little antelopes drink regularly. They are much more dependent on water than other antelopes and seldom live far from it. The edge of the jungle round a village tank is a favourite resort. Again, unlike antelopes they do not gather in large herds. *Chousingha* are usually seen alone or in pairs. In the early part of the year, before the rains, the female may be accompanied by one or two fawns. Sometimes two old animals and two young will be seen together, or even a buck with 4 or 5 does.

The Four-horned Antelope is found along the base of the Himalayas. It does not occur in the Gangetic plain. In the peninsula of India it has a more or less localised distribution. Here it keeps to the hill tracts covered with open forest. It is not found on the Malabar coast.

THE NILGAI OR BLUE BULL (*BOSELAPHUS TRAGOCAMELUS* PALL.).

The Nilgai is a great ungainly antelope standing fully 54 in. at the shoulder and weighing about 600 lbs.

Its high withers and low hind quarters recall the build of the African Hartebeeste. As is usual with so many African Tragelaphines, the sexes differ in colour.

The adult bull has a coarse iron grey coat. He has a white ring below each fetlock and two white spots on each cheek. His lips, chin, the inside of his ears and the undersurface of his tail are white. Young bulls and the cows are tawny. Both sexes have dark manes and the males wear a distinctive tuft of stiff black hairs on the throat. The bulls have stout cone-like horns. They are distinctly keeled, triangular at the base and circular towards the tips.

Horns average about 8 in. The maximum length is $11\frac{3}{4}$ in.

Nilgai are usually seen in herds of 10-15 animals. Males are often solitary or perhaps several bulls will herd together. Females and young, attended or not, by one or two old males may be seen in smaller or larger parties. The country they live in may be level, undulating or hilly. They favour a mixture of grassland, scrub and cultivation, usually avoid really dense forest but will live in more or less open tree jungle.

They feed on grass and cereal crops and browse on leaves and wild fruit and are particularly fond of eating the fallen flowers of the Mowha tree. They feed at all times of the day.

When alarmed the herd goes off with an ungainly slouching gallop covering the most difficult ground with ease.

Nilgai droppings are commonly found heaped in one particular spot. This habit is common in many animals. It is suggested that the spot may provide *rendezvous* for reassembling the scattered members of a herd.

The period of gestation is 8-9 months. Young are seen at all seasons.

The Nilgai is found in the Indian Peninsula from the base of the Himalayas to Mysore. It does not occur in Eastern Bengal or Assam or on the Malabar coast. The sanctity attributed to it is the main source of its protection in many districts where it has survived.

Family II. *CERVIDAE* OR DEER.

The last tribe of true ruminants is the Deer. Branching horns or antlers are the distinctive appanage of deer. Save in one or two aberrant forms only males carry them. In the Reindeer alone both sexes are horned. Deer, like other ruminants, are generally large and heavy creatures without the agility and litheness of beasts of prey. It is precisely to this sort of animal, where weight is an important factor, that horns are the most suitable weapons. They are perhaps a counterpoise to the teeth and claws of Carnivores. The need for defence against enemies, for weapons of attack in combats with their own kind has led to this distinctive form of protective armament among hoofed animals. But there is a distinction between the horns of oxen, sheep and antelopes and the deer tribe. A deer's horn when fully developed is really a mass of dead bone, devoid of any covering of skin or horn. The antlers are worn for a time, shed and then replaced. The budding antler grows from a pedestal or pedicel of bone which forms part of the skull. It appears as a velvety knob, grows rapidly, increasing in length by the vigorous deposition of bony matter. In young deer it remains a simple spike. In adult stags it branches into tines and takes the form of the complete antler. The new grown antler is highly sensitive. It is covered with 'velvet'—a thick soft skin, fed by numerous blood vessels and clothed with a mat of fine hair. When the growth of the antler is complete, a ring of bony matter, the 'burr', forms at its base just above its union with the pedicle. The bony ring constricts and cuts off the flow of blood to the antler. The blood vessels in the 'velvet' dry up. The 'velvet' shrinks and is eventually rubbed away by the deer. When present, it takes the place of the horny sheath which forms a permanent cover over the bony cores of the horns of cattle and other hollow-horned ruminants. But in the deer the outer cover of the antler is temporary. It is removed and leaves behind the dead bone which we call horn.

Besides the antlers, there are other characters which distinguish deer from other ruminants. Deer have a large fissure in the skull just in advance of the eye socket. As a rule canine teeth are present in the upper jaw. They are particularly well developed in forms which have no antlers such as Musk deer and Chevrotains.

Again, with the exception of the Musk deer, none of the tribe have a gall bladder. All deer have well developed lateral hoofs in both feet. The tribe ranges over a great part of Asia, North and South America and North-West Africa.

Sub-Family I. *Moschinae*: Musk Deer.

THE MUSK DEER (*MOSCHUS MOSCHIFEROUS* L.).

The Deer tribe is divided into two groups or sub-families—the *Moschinae*, containing a single genus and species the Musk deer and the *Cervinae* which includes all the remaining deer. The Musk Deer holds a place between the deer and the antelopes. It is regarded as an undeveloped form of deer which has not progressed with the rest of its tribe. It is hornless, has no face glands; these are generally present in all deer, and it has a gall bladder which no deer possesses. In some ways it has taken a special line of development of its own. This is seen in its possession of a caudal gland and a musk gland. The tail of a musk deer is peculiar. It is completely buried in the long hairs of the anal region and is for the most part naked except for a large tuft at the tip and a tuft at the base which covers its upper surface and sides. The lateral surface of the tail bears a narrow slit in its flacid skin which is the opening of the caudal gland. The musk gland is situated beneath the skin of the abdomen of the males. When fresh its secretion has an unpleasant pungent, urinary odour, when dry it acquires the scent of musk. Valued as a commercial product it induces the persecution of the species. From the great development of the caudal and musk glands it is inferred that in this deer the females seek out the males in the breeding season. Finally, musk deer have specially mobile feet, the hoofs are long and pointed and the unusually large lateral hoofs are well adapted to give it a foothold on snowy slopes and slippery rocks. The absence of horns is compensated by the great development of the canine teeth.

The Musk Deer is a little creature standing 20 in. at the shoulder and weighing as many lbs. It is protected from the cold by a deep coat of thick and bristly hairs, almost pithy in structure. The general colour is a shade of rich dark brown speckled with grey. It lives singly or in pairs. Musk deer are generally met with in birch forest above the zone of the pines, at times they come down to lower levels but always keep in thick cover. They scrape out a shallow form in which they lie concealed and come out to feed in the mornings and evenings.

The breeding season is believed to be in January and the young are born in June. Musk Deer range over a wide area in Central and North Eastern Asia. The typical form *Moschus moschiferous* is found in Kashmir, Nepal and Sikhim.

Sub-Family II. *Cervinae*: Deer.

THE MUNTJAC (*MUNTIACUS MUNTJAK* ZIMM.).

The second division of the Deer tribe—the *Cervinae* contains all the remaining deer. True deer have no gall bladder, no caudal or musk glands—all present in musk deer. With the exception of Roe deer, all deer have face glands. Again, all, save the Chinese water deer, have antlers and all of them, except the little Pudu deer of the Chilian Andes, have foot glands. The group contains 19 genera six of which are present in our area.

The Muntjacs, known also as Barking Deer, are small animals standing from 20-30 in. at the shoulder. The antlers are small. They consist of a short brow tine and a beam which is undivided and curves downwards and inwards at its extremity. The horns are set on long bony pedicels. A bony ridge extends down each side of the face from the base of each pedicel. The marked prominence of the facial ridges gives the creature the name 'rib-faced deer'. In females there is a bristly tuft of hair and a small projection in place of each horn.

Muntjacs range over the greater part of the Indo Malayan countries and are found also in China, Formosa and Japan. Various races are recognised over this wide range.

In our area there are supposed to be three: the Muntjac of North India is known as (*Muntiacus m. vaginalis*); the southern form is (*M. m. aureus*). The third race (*M. m. grandicornis*) is found in Burma. The Muntjac of Tenasserim (*M. feae*) is regarded as a distinct species. The coat of the Burmese Muntjac is described as tawny yellow; the North Indian race is bright chestnut. A bright red form is equally common in Burma. The antlers of an adult male in Burma average 4 in., their bony pedicels measuring from 2-4 in. The best Burmese head is 7 in. Average Indian antlers measure from 2-3 in. The pedicel 3-4 in. The maximum length obtained in the C.P. is 7 in. A good buck weighs from 48-50 lbs. Horns are shed during May and June. The Muntjac is a solitary animal. It is seen singly or in pairs; more rarely, in small family parties. It keeps to more or less thick jungle and comes out to graze in the outskirts of forest or in open clearings. It is fairly diurnal in habit. The food consists of various leaves and grasses and wild fruits. Its call from a distance sounds much like the bark of a dog. It is given out at intervals; usually in the mornings and evenings, sometimes after nightfall.

When alarmed and in flight these deer give out a series of short cackling barks which may be reduced to a sharp rattle likened to the sound of castanets. Muntjac appear to breed at all seasons. The rut mainly takes place in the cold weather. The young usually one—sometimes two, are born at the beginning of the rains. The young are spotted white till about 6 months old.

THE CHITAL OR SPOTTED DEER (*AXIS AXIS* EXRL.).

The Chital, perhaps the most beautiful of all deer, is found only in India and Ceylon. In India, it is found in the forests at the base of the Himalayas and practically throughout the peninsula wherever there is more or less open jungle combined with good grazing and a plentiful supply of water. It is unknown in the arid plains of the Punjab, Sind, in a large portion of Rajputana, in Assam and the countries east of the Bay of Bengal.

The Spotted Deer is at its best in the Himalayan foot hills, in the jungles of the Terai and in the Central Provinces. A well-built stag from these parts stands 36 in. at the shoulder and weighs about 190 lbs.

In South India, or in the jungles of the Sunderbans, the height seldom exceeds 2 ft. 6 in. The coat is a bright rufous fawn profusely spotted with white. The lower series of spots on the flanks are arranged in longitudinal rows and suggest broken linear marking. Its dappled hide almost obliterates the chital in a sun-flecked jungle, particularly when it sits down to rest as it usually does, in some shady place.

The graceful antlers have 3 tines—a long brow tine set nearly at right angles to the beam and two branch tines at the top. The outer tine, the continuation of the beam, is always the longer.

The record head measures 39¾ in. A 34 in. antler would be good anywhere; 31 in. in South India.

One always associates Chital with beautiful scenery, with grassy forest glades and shaded streams. They are seen in herds of ten to thirty, which may contain two or three stags; but assemblages numbering several hundred have been met with. They do not shun the proximity of villages, enter cultivation and frequently associate with many forest animals, particularly with monkeys. They are less nocturnal than sambar and feed till late in the morning and again in the afternoon, and lie down in the interval in some shaded spot.

The time at which the stags shed their antlers varies in different localities. In the Central Provinces and South India, as a rule, stags cast their horns in August and September. The new antlers are in velvet till the end of December. But stags carrying horns in various stages of development have been seen at all seasons. It is suggested that regularity in the intervals at which antlers are shed is only attained by fully mature stags. In the Central Provinces, the pairing season is at its height in May. The rutting stag has a loud harsh bellow and combats between males for the possession of the hinds are fierce and frequent. In North India the pairing is said to take place during the winter months. Fawns may be met with at any season. One to three are born at a time —two being the commoner number. Chital are prolific breeders; an interval of 6 months may see the production of a new family.

THE HOG DEER (*HYELAPHUS PORCINUS* ZIMM.).

The name Hog Deer has been probably suggested by the squat pig-like appearance of this animal and by its hog-like movements. When running it keeps its head low down, moves without that bounding action so characteristic in deer.

The Hog Deer is a relative of the Chital but is smaller and stouter in build. The body is long and the legs relatively short. The height at the withers is about 27-29 in. The fur is brown, dark brown in old stags, with a yellowish or reddish tinge. The white tips to the individual hairs give the coat a speckly appearance. The under parts of the body are paler and the inside of the ears and the underside of the tail are white. The young are spotted. Some young stags and hinds show these spots though they are not always discernible. The summer coat is generally paler.

The small antlers are set upon very long bony pedicels. After giving out a short brow tine the beam is almost straight till it divides into a shorter fore and longer hind tine. Average horns measure from 12-15 in. Burmese stags carry better heads than Indian. The record is 24 in. Hog deer favour grass jungles by the banks or rivers, grass-covered delta islands or open grass plains; always where the grass is not too high. On the banks of the Indus in Upper Sind they live in scrub jungle and in Burma, they were once common in mangroves. Hog Deer are generally solitary creatures. A pair will continue to frequent a particular stretch of grassland. Sometimes small parties of 2-5 may be found grazing together. They come out to feed early in the mornings and in the evenings, and shelter in long grass during the hot hours of the day. They are wary creatures; their sense of sight, smell and hearing is acute. Persecution has made them almost nocturnal in many parts of their range.

The main pairing season is believed to be in September and October and the young are dropped in April and May. Pairing must also take place earlier in the year as young are often born during the rains. The period of gestation is 8 months. The Hog Deer is not found in the Indian Peninsula. It lives in the low alluvial grass plains of North India from Sind and the Punjab to Assam whence its range extends into Burma and Tenasserim.

THE SAMBAR (*RUSA UNICOLOR* KERR.).

The Sambar is the typical forest deer of South Eastern Asia. In the Indian Empire it is represented by the Indian Sambar (*Rusa unicolor*), whose range includes Ceylon and by the Malay Sambar (*Rusa unicolor equinus*), which inhabits Assam, Burma and the Malay countries.

Of the many races of Sambar, the Indian is the largest and carries the grandest horns. It is a heavily built deer which may reach a shoulder height of nearly 5 ft. The average height is about 55 in. A full grown stag scales from 500-600 lbs. The coat is coarse and shaggy. In stags it forms a mane about the neck and throat. In the hot weather much of the hair is shed. The general colour is brown with a yellowish or greyish tinge. The under parts are paler. Females are lighter in tone. Old stags tend to grow very dark—almost black. The antlers are stout and rugged. The brow tine is set at an acute angle with the beam. At its summit, the beam forks into two nearly equal tines. In some heads the outer, in others the inner tine is longer. The full number of points are developed in the fourth year. The Sambar stag is said to be at its prime in its ninth year. Really old beasts carry poor heads. Sambar from the Himalayan foot hills have more rugose and perhaps more massive antlers than those of the C.P., but they are never so long or so graceful. The finest heads come from the forests about the Narbada and Tapti and from the Central Provinces generally. The record is the famous head from Bhopal which tapes $50\frac{7}{8}$ in. The horns of the Malay Sambar are set closer. They have a more rugged and massive appearance. The average length is 26 in. A head over 30 in. is good.

Forested hill sides, preferably near cultivation, are the favourite haunt of Sambar. Their food consists of grass, leaves and various kinds of wild fruit. They feed mainly at night and retire into heavy cover at day-break and do not come out till dusk. The capacity of so heavy an animal to move silently through dense jungle is amazing. Their powers of sight are moderate; their scent and hearing acute. Sambar take to water readily and swim with the body submerged only the face and the antler showing above the surface. There is much variation both as to the pairing season and the time at which the antlers are shed. Stags in velvet and others with mature horns are seen together. In Central and Southern India the majority of stags cast their antlers between the end of March and mid-April. The horns commence to grow in May and are in velvet during the rains. In September, the stags commence to clean their horns by rubbing them against trees. The tree is taken between the brow tine and beam and the antler is rubbed up and down leaving a long blaze on the bark. Most of the stags are clear of velvet by November. They roar in challenge to each other. The challenge is a loud metallic bellow quite distinct from sharp short 'ponk' which is the alarm note. The males fight for territory. Each stag fights to obtain sole rights over some favoured valley. The victor becomes master of the hinds which enter it. The hinds are attracted to the stags by their calls and the scent of the face glands, which are everted during the rut and give out their strong smelling secretion. Pairing takes place in November and December. The stag's harem is limited to a few hinds. After the rut he deserts them and lives a solitary life till the return of the mating season. The young are born at the commencement of the rains, in late May or early June. Young stags remain with the hinds. Sambar are rarely found associating in large numbers. Four or five to dozen are what one usually sees. Both stags and hinds are seen singly or a party of hinds and fawns without a stag.

THE SWAMP DEER (*RUCERVUS DUVAUCELLI* CUV.).

The Swamp Deer group, forming the genus *Rucervus* contains three species within our area:—The Swamp Deer (*Rucervus duvaucelli*), Eld's Deer (*Rucervus eldi*) of Manipur and the Thamin (*Rucervus thamin*) of Burma.

The Swamp Deer—the *Barasingh* of the Central Provinces and the *Gond* of the United Provinces and Terai is found in the Central Provinces, the United Provinces, parts of Assam and the Sunderbans. Its occurrence in Sind is doubted.

This splendid deer attains its finest development in the Central Provinces. A good stag stands 54 in. at the shoulder and scales from 370-400 lbs. Its coat almost woolly in texture shades from brown to yellowish brown. The stags are maned and darker in colour. The summer coat of stags and hinds is paler, some develop spots, not always distinct, of lighter tone. The young are spotted.

There is much variation in the form of the antlers. Two distinct types are recognised with a wide range of intermediary patterns. In the first form, the beam takes a backward and then forward curve bringing the points of the horns in line with the top of the head. Half way up the beam, tines are given off at intervals: the first usually having a shoot of its own. In the second and far handsomer type, the brow tine is set at right angles to the beam, which grows with an outward curve giving the antlers a wider spread. At the point where it branches, the beam takes an almost horizontal curve and gives off number of vigorous vertical tines each of which throws out shoots. The whole effect is to produce an extraordinarily beautiful form of antler. Antlers from the Terai are smoother and whiter than C. P. heads. Heads exceeding 41 in. are rare. 10-14 is the usual number of points, though antlers with as many as twenty points have been obtained. The term Swamp Deer exactly suits the animal in the Terai where it lives in marsh land and is seldom out of water. In the Central Provinces this deer lives in grassy plains on hard ground and is, on the whole, less dependent on the proximity of water than the Chital. In Assam they usually live in high ground in the proximity of water. Swamp Deer are highly gregarious. In parts of the Terai a few miles of swamp may contain thousands of these magnificent animals. Swamp deer are less nocturnal than Sambar. They feed till late in the morning, again in the evening and lie up during the day. Their eyesight and hearing is moderate. The sense of smell acute. When alarmed the whole herd sets up a shrill baying sound which is continued in flight. In Assam the antlers are shed in February and March. The new antlers appear between April and May. They are in velvet till the end of July and are clean by the end of September. In the U.P. and C.P. stags are hornless by mid-April. Horns are mostly in velvet between May and August. They harden in September and are generally clear of velvet by mid-October. The master stags assemble.

Their eerie and penetrating roars are thrilling and impressive. They live more or less in amity till the rut develops. In the C.P. this is mainly between mid-December and mid-January. In the U.P. the chief rutting season is in November and December. The males fight for the possession of the hinds and each master stag so acquires his harem which may number as many as 30 hinds. It is reported that in Assam the pairing season is in April and May when the stags' new antlers are beginning to sprout!

With the cooling of their short-lived ardour the stags desert the hinds. The master stags collect again in small herds. The younger males remain with the hinds. The finest stags go off to live alone or in company with another of equal development. The young are born just before the rains. In Assam the young are born mainly between December and January or as late as February.

THE THAMIN OR BROW-ANTLERED DEER (*RUCERVUS THAMIN* THOS.).

The Thamin, the typical deer of Burma, is found mainly in the dry zone of Central Burma. It is sparingly distributed in other parts of the Province. It was once found in immense numbers in the wide plains of Pegu.

This beautiful deer is nearly 4 ft. high at the withers. The hinds are smaller. The coat is coarse and sparse. In stags it is dark brown or nearly black. Stags have a dense mane or ruff about the throat. Hinds are a light fawn. The young are spotted. There appears to be a seasonal colour change; the dark brown thamin of the cold season developing into the yellowish brown animals of the hot weather. The close set antlers are very handsome. In profile their form is almost circular. From the tip of the brow tine to the point of the beam the antler sweeps in one continuous, graceful curve. The number of terminal tines varies from two or three to as many as eight or ten. There are supposed to be two races of Thamin in Burma. The typical thamin and Bruce's Thamin (*R. thamin brucci*), described from the Ruby Mines District, in which the horns are said to be slightly palmated. The maximum length of the antlers is 42 in. Heads over 35 in. are good. Stags are believed to acquire their horns in the second year and reach their prime when 7 years old.

Thamin avoid hills or heavy forest. These Deer prefer open scrub jungle on flat or undulating land between rivers and hill ranges. They live in small herds, lying up in cover during the heat of the day and feeding in the mornings and evenings. After nightfall, they come out to graze in the large *lwins* and *kwins* or to raid crops in their vicinity. Their speed and sharp sight is their main protection.

Stags shed their antlers in mid-August and are clear of velvet by the end of December, when the horns are at their best. The rut develops between March and April. The period of gestation is 8 months. The fawns, one at birth, are dropped mostly in October. After the rut the master stags go off either alone or attended by one or two hinds. Big stags are seldom seen with the herds after May.

Eld's Deer (*Rucervus eldi*) is confined to Manipur where it lives in grassy swamps. Its antlers are indistinguishable from the Thamin. The hind pasterns are horny instead of hairy and applied to the ground when walking.

Thamin have suffered much from persecution in Burma. Without effective measures for their protection this beautiful deer must face extinction.

THE KASHMIR STAG OR HANGUL (*CERVUS CASHMIRIENSIS* FALC.).

The Red Deer of Europe typifies a group of large deer consisting of several species and varieties distributed over Europe, Asia, north of the Himalayas, North Africa and North America. The best known Asiatic species is the *Hangul* or Kashmir Stag. Its range is limited to the north side of the valley of Kashmir and some of the adjacent valleys.

The Kashmir Stag is smaller than the Sambar. It is from 48-50 in. high at the withers. A well grown stag scales a little over 400 lbs. The coat ranges from light to dark brown, fading to dingy white on the lips, chin, underparts and buttocks. The colour fades during the summer but tones up with the denser winter coat, which, in a big stag, is very dark or rufous brown. Fawns are spotted. Old hinds may show white flecks. The fine spreading antlers assume great variety in form. Normal heads have 5 points on each antler. Heads with 16 points have been obtained, 14 pointers are rare; 13 and 11 more common.

The Kashmir Stag is essentially a forest animal. These deer are found singly or in small parties. They seldom remain long in one area but roam from forest to forest to find good grazing. Stags shed their antlers between mid-March and April. Young stags may carry their horns upto the middle of May. After shedding their antlers most stags go up hill and congregate about the snow line. They spend the summer at an elevation of 9,000 to 12,000 ft. About the end of September the stags' new antlers have hardened. They commence to roar and challenge. They join the hinds at the beginning of October and, as the rut develops, engage in conflict. The master stags collect a number of hinds whose possession is disputed by rivals. In November, when the dry leaves cover the ground, the stags desert the hinds and go to the upland meadows or into the horse-chestnut forests. In hard winters the deer descend to lower levels. They come to the lower elevations in the early spring to feed on the new sprouting grass and the budding larches. The fawns are born in April.

The Chumbi Valley in Tibet and some of the adjacent valleys of Bhutan are inhabited by another species of the Red Deer group —the Shou (*Cervus affinis*). It is also called the Sikhim Stag though its existence in Sikhim is doubted. The Shou is much larger than the Hangul, standing from 4½ to 5 ft. at the shoulder. Its antlers are longer and more massive. Their distinctive feature is the forward bend of the beam at the junction of the third tine.

SECTION *TRAGULINA.*

CHEVROTAINS OR MOUSE DEER.

The cloven-hoofed animals which we have considered so far all belong to one great division—the *Pecora* or Ruminants. The Mouse Deer represent a second division. They are true ruminants and, like ruminants, have no front teeth in the upper jaw. But they differ in having a three-chambered stomach in place of one with four divisions. They have four well-developed toes on each foot, the bones of the petty or side toes being complete. In true ruminants some of these bones are imperfect or wanting. Antlers are not developed. Mouse Deer, like Musk Deer, are furnished with tusks. These are better developed in males. Mouse Deer are included in a single family the *Tragulidae* which contains three genera: (1) The Indian Chevrotain (*Moschiola*), (2) The Malay Chevrotains (*Tragulus*) and (3) The African Water Chevrotain (*Hyemoschus*). The Asiatic Chevrotains are distinguished from the African by having true cannon bones developed.

The Indian Chevrotain or Mouse Deer (*Moschiola meminna*) is a tiny little creature no more than 10 or 11 in. high. Because of its small size, shy habits and very protective colouring it easily escapes observation. Its coat is olive brown speckled with yellow. The flanks are marked with rows of buff or white spots. The lower parts are white. The throat has three white stripes. The Malay Chevrotains are distinguished from the Indian by having the skin on the chin and throat naked instead of hairy. Their coats are not spotted. There are two species in Burma—the larger Malay Chevrotain (*Tragulus canescens*) and the Lesser Malay Chevrotain (*Tragulus kanchil ravus*). The former is about 28 in. long and 13 in. high, the latter is no longer than 18 in. from the tip of the nose to the root of the tail. The smaller animal has three white stripes on its throat, the larger five. Both species are common in the forests of Tenasserim.

All Chevrotain have similar habits. The Indian Mouse Deer shelters in grass covered rocky hillsides or in forest. It conceals itself in the crevices of rocks or among large boulders, coming out to feed in the mornings or evenings and never venturing far out into the open. In these 'hides' the female brings forth her young, generally two in number, at the end of the rains or the commencement of the cold season. The males live solitary except during the pairing season. The Indian species is found in Central and Southern India. The Malay species live in dense thickets. Like the Indian species they pair in June or July.

SECTION *SUINA*.

PIGS, PECCARIES AND HIPPOPOTAMUSES.

The Chevrotains represent, as was shown, a group of animals somewhat distinct from the true ruminants. Pigs, Peccaries and Hippopotamuses are a stage yet further removed from typical ruminants. They form a third section of the *Artiodactyla*. Their feet, like the feet of the Chevrotains, have the bones of the 4 toes complete. All these pig-like animals have incisor teeth in the upper jaws. Their molar teeth when unworn are capped with small hillock-like columns which do not wear down to crescentic patterns seen in the grinding teeth of ruminants. As they are not ruminants their stomachs are much less complex and may, as in the pigs, consist of a single chamber.

Finally, cannon bones are not developed in the feet, the bones which fuse to form a cannon bone in true ruminants remain distinct in these animals. These pig-like animals represent a more primitive type which existed at a time when ruminants were unknown and which formed the ancestral stock from which they have descended.

The Peccaries are exclusively American in their distribution. Hippopotami are now limited to Africa but many species once inhabited India. They were probably contemporary with the Stone Age Man in this country.

The Pigs (*Suidae*) are the only representatives of the division in our area. There are two genera: (1) the Wild Boar (*Sus*) and (2) the Pigmy Hog (*Porcula*). An elongate head with an abruptly truncated mobile snout, ending in a flat disc containing the nostrils is distinctive in pigs. Their feet are narrow. The petty toes are completely developed but do not reach the ground when walking. The upper canines curve upwards and outwards.

The Pigmy Hog is closely related to the typical Pigs. On account of its small size, short tail and the presence of three pairs of teats instead of 4, it is regarded as a separate genus. Though a single species of wild boar is now found in India, in the Eocene Period six or seven species inhabited the country—one of them a monster form, the largest known of its race.

Family IV. *SUIDAE*, PIGS.

THE INDIAN WILD BOAR (*SUS CRISTATUS* WAGN.).

The Indian Wild Boar is widely distributed. It ranges over nearly the whole of India, Burma and Tenasserim, Siam and part of the Malay Peninsula. It is also found in Ceylon.

A well grown male stands about 36 in. at the shoulder. It is believed to be a larger animal than the European Boar with a sparser coat and a fuller crest or mane. The weight of an adult may well exceed 300 lbs. The tusks are well developed in the males both the upper and lower curve outwards and project from the mouth. The lower tusks in a large boar are said to have measured 12 in. including the portion embedded in the jaw. But they rarely exceed 9 in.

The tame pig of India is probably derived from the wild. The two probably interbreed when opportunity offers. The colour is black mixed with grey, rusty-brown and white hairs. The young are browner and old boars greyer. New born wild pigs are brown with light or dark stripes.

The Indian Wild Boar lives in grass or scanty bush jungle—sometimes in forest; after the rains, quite commonly in high crops. They are omnivorous living on crops, roots, tubers, insects, snakes, offal and carrion. They feed in the early mornings and late in the evening and, where much disturbed, chiefly at night. No animal is more destructive to crops and, in cultivated areas, it is impossible to make a plea for its protection.

Wild Boar display great intelligence, and few animals show greater courage and determination. The sense of smell is acute, the eyesight and hearing moderate. Wild Boar are highly prolific. They apparently breed at all season. In Central India the majority of young are born at two periods shortly before or after the rains. Boars and sows are known to collect in large assemblies when pairing. A herd of 170 or more were seen by Mr. Dunbar Brander. They were collected in a circle, the master boars in the centre. Two males were fighting—two others had fought; the rest were passive though interested spectators. The period of gestation is said to be four months—4-6 young are born at a time. The mother shelters them in a heaped up mass of grass or branches which she builds before she litters.

After breeding the big boars live alone or in company with another of equal size or with one or two sows.

The Pigmy Hog (*Porcula salvania*) inhabits the forests at the base of the Himalayas in Sikhim, Nepal, Bhutan and in Assam. Its habits are similar to those of Wild Pig. It is said to live in herds of 5-20. It is nocturnal and rarely seen.

PERISSODACTYLA: ODD-TOED UNGULATES.

It has been shown that there are four main divisions or Orders of hoofed animals and that all those considered so far, belong to the first and largest division the Artiodactyla or Even-toed Ungulates The salient feature which distinguishes the even-toed ungulate lies in the arrangement of its toes. The axis of the foot—a line drawn down its middle—passes between the third and fourth toes. These two toes are large and equal in size. The hoofs which encase them appear like a single hoof cleft in two. This prominence of the third and fourth toe is accompanied by the diminishing in size of the second and fifth and the complete disappearance of the first toe. This is the general plan of structure in the feet of oxen, sheep, goats, deer and pigs.

With Horses, Rhinoceroses and Tapirs we come to an assemblage of animals differing in many important respects from those so far described. Their most obvious distinction is again displayed in the structure of the feet. Like the even-toed ungulates they are descendants of 5-toed ancestors. But with them it is the third or middle toe of the foot which has increased in size at the expense of the others. The number of toes varies. A Tapir has four and a Rhinoceros three toes on the fore feet. Both have only three on the hind. The foot of a horse has but one functional toe. But in all these animals it is the third or the middle toe of the foot which is most prominent. It is always symmetrical in itself and always larger than the other toes, when these are present. This pre-eminence of the third or middle digit of the foot gives this group of animals its name—*Perissodactyla* or Odd-toed Ungulates. With them, except in the case of the Tapirs, the number of toes in each foot is usually odd—either one or three. The Odd-toed ungulates are further marked by having their molar and pre-molar teeth in one unbroken series, the posterior molars resembling the pre-molars in shape and size.

The Odd-toed ungulates are poorly represented at the present day. Horses, Rhinoceroses and Tapirs are the only surviving members of a group of animals which flourished in great variety during the earlier Tertiary period. With the exception of the Tapirs which are found also in Central and South America all the existing odd-toed ungulates are Old World animals.

Family I: *EQUIDAE*.

HORSES, ASSES AND ZEBRAS.

THE KIANG (*Equus kiang* Moorcroft.).

THE GHOR-KHAR OR INDIAN WILD ASS (*Equus onager indicus* Blyth.).

The Horse tribe includes the Asses and Zebras. In all these animals each foot has a single complete toe encased in a large solid hoof. It is supported by a long bone known as the 'cannon bone'. Small splint bones on each side of the 'cannon' bone represent the vestiges of the second and fourth toes. The cheek teeth are large, quadrangular and complex, the enamel foldings being numerous as compared with the simpler ones of the Rhinoceroses and Tapir.

In the wild state the family is confined to the plains of Asia and Africa. Two species are resident in our area. The Kiang (*Equus kiang*) and the Ghor-khar or Indian Wild Ass (*E. onager indicus*). The Kiang lives in the high open plateaus of Ladak and Tibet. The Indian Wild Ass is found in Baluchistan, Cutch and in parts of the desert zone of North-Western India. Both the Kiang and the Ghor-khar are more closely allied to the Horse than to the true wild asses of North Africa. Like all Wild Asses, they have short upright manes. Those curious callosities seen on the inside of the legs of the horse, the purpose of which is unknown are absent in the ass. The Kiang is distinguished by its large horse-like hoofs. The hoofs of the Ghor-khar are smaller and more ass-like. A Kiang's ears are comparatively short. The coat is reddish in summer, tawny grey, woolly and dense in winter. Like all wild asses it has a dark brown stripe along the back from the nape to the tail. A Kiang stands about 51-52 in. at the shoulder.

Wild asses are usually shy and difficult to approach but the Kiang is one of the most inquisitive of animals and will frequently approach within 50 yards or so of any strange object.

The Ghor-khar which is the eastern race of the Persian Wild Ass is a smaller animal than the Kiang. It is about 46 in. high at the shoulder. In summer its coat is sandy, in winter, grey.

Wild asses are remarkable for their fleetness and their capacity of getting over rough and stony ground at a great pace. As a rule these animals inhabit desert plains or as in the case of the Kiang open rolling tablelands where both desert and arctic conditions prevail.

They associate in small parties of 4 or 5. Sometimes these parties unite and form large herds. During the foaling time the Kiang mares collect in certain favoured areas while the stallions are scattered about either solitary or in twos and threes.

In the plains to the west of the Indus, Wild Asses are found wandering about for the greater part of the year but in the hot weather when the grass withers and water is scarce they migrate to the hills. The mares are said to drop their foals in July and August.

Family II: *RHINOCEROTIDAE* RHINOCEROSES.

The various species of Rhinoceroses, all now confined to the Old World, differ remarkably from one another in structure. As a result of migrations during past epochs into different habitats and climates, into new feeding grounds to which they became adapted, the various species appear to have become distinct at a very early period of their history.

A comparison of the remains of numerous extinct forms with those now living indicates 7 distinct lines of descent and evolution from which lesser branches were given off. Though these animals are externally similar they are thus really very far apart both in history and anatomy: even the two living African Rhinoceroses probably separated from each other and became distinct species a million years ago.

Three species of Rhinoceros are found within our limits. The Great One-horned Rhinoceros (*Rhinoceros indicus*) and its relative, the Smaller One-horned or Javan Rhinoceros (*Rhinoceros sondaicus*) have an obscure genealogical history. No representatives of these true and typical Rhinoceroses have been discovered anywhere but in South-Eastern Asia. Their remains are not found in the more ancient Sivalik beds. But they appear with relative suddenness in the uppermost and more recent beds in the form of two species known as the Sivalik Rhinoceros (*R. sivalensis*) and *R. palaeindicus* the ancient Rhinoceros of India.

The Asiatic two-horned Rhinoceros (*R. sumatrensis*) was on the other hand widely distributed in the past. It was quite abundant in the Sivalik hills in Pliocene times. It was a geological period when these animals, favoured by a genial climate, inhabited a broad forest belt which stretched from the east coast of England southwards and eastward across Southern France and North Italy to India.

All the living Rhinoceroses are included in a single genus. Their massive build, the thickness and solidity of their bones, their short stumpy legs each furnished with three toes are some of the family characters. The skin in all the living forms is either thinly clad with hair or naked and in all the Indian species the heavy hide in places is thrown into deep folds. The nasal bones are enlarged to serve as a support for a single or double horns. When two horns are present they are situated one behind the other in the middle line of the snout. The horn is formed of a closely matted mass of horny fibre issuing from the skin. It has no connection with the skull, although a supporting boss of bone in the skull may serve as its foundation.

The horns grow throughout life and if lost are reproduced.

THE GREAT ONE-HORNED RHINOCEROS (*RHINOCEROS UNICORNIS* L.).

The Great Indian Rhinoceros, probably the largest of all living Rhinoceroses may reach over 6 ft. at the shoulder.

The average height of a well-grown animal is about 5 ft. 8 in. with a girth of 11 ft. behind the shoulder. The skin of this massive creature is divided into great shields by heavy folds before and behind the shoulder and in front of the thighs. In this Rhinoceros the folding of the skin in front of the shoulders is not continued right across the back. The skin on the flanks, shoulders and hind quarters, is covered with a mass of rounded tubercles. With his grotesque shape, long boat-shaped head, his folds of armour, his scaly hide he looks like a monster of some byegone age. The horns of the Indian Rhinoceros never compare with those of the African. The record from Assam measures 24 in. 15-16 in. is a good average length.

The males may be recognised from the females by a shorter and thicker horn blunted by frequent combats. The female's horn is sharper and longer. Though it prefers swamp and grass the Great Indian Rhinoceros is also found in wood jungle up ravines and low hills.

The animal is solitary as a rule though several may occupy the same patch of jungle. Along the numerous rivers which flow through the jungles of the Nepal Terai the rhino has particular places for dropping its excreta. Mounds so accumulate in places. In approaching these spots a rhinoceros walks backwards and falls an easy victim to poachers. Breeding takes place at all times of the year. The period of gestation is given as 17 to 18 months. In Nepal it is generally believed to be one year. A fully developed calf taken from the uterus measured 4 ft. 1 in. and scaled 120 lbs.

The food consists chiefly of grass. In Nepal during the rains Rhinoceros frequently enter cultivation. Many legends and beliefs are attached to this animal. In Europe, during the Middle Ages its horn was generally believed to have peculiar medicinal virtues.

In Nepal the flesh and the blood of the Rhinoceros is considered highly acceptable to the *Manes*. High caste Hindus and most Gurkhas offer libation of the animal's blood after entering its disembowelled body. On ordinary *Sradh* days the libation of water and milk is poured from a cup carved from its horn. The urine is considered antiseptic and is hung in a vessel at the principal door as a charm against ghosts, evil spirits and diseases. These beliefs connected with the Rhinoceros are prevalent in varying form in Burma, Siam and China. They set a great value upon the animal and provide the main reason for its persecution. In Nepal, the Indian Rhinoceros is found only in the country to the east of the Gandak river known as Chitawan where strict preservation by the Nepal Government has saved it from extinction. In parts of Assam, where it is still found, strict preservation has temporarily saved it from extermination.

THE SMALLER ONE-HORNED OR JAVAN RHINOCEROS (*RHINOCEROS SONDAICUS* CUV.).

The Javan Rhinoceros is a close relative of the Great One-horned Rhinoceros. Though smaller, it is still a very bulky animal. Old bulls measure about 5 ft. 10 in. at the shoulder. The single horn is never very long. 10¾ in. is the record. The horn does not appear to be developed in females or, if developed at all, it is only a low boss. In distinction to its relative, the fold of skin on the shoulders is continued across the back. The hide is marked all over with a mosaic like pattern.

The Smaller One-horned Rhinoceros was once believed to range from Bengal and Assam through Burma and the Malay Peninsula to Sumatra. As far as can be ascertained its range is now limited to the Malay Peninsula and Java where a few still exist under protection. In earlier works on Burma, it is mentioned as having been once abundant in the forested banks of large rivers in the district of Tenasserim. Recent attempts to discover whether this rhinoceros still exists in Burma have failed and it is doubted whether there are more than half a dozen specimens and it is doubtful whether these will survive without adequate measures for their protection. Though it occurred in the Bengal Duars in former years, its presence in this area at the present time requires verification.

The Smaller One-horned Rhinoceros is more an inhabitant of tree forest than of grass land. Its low crowned grinding teeth indicate that it is a browser, indulging less in grazing than the Indian Rhinoceros, whose armoury of high crowned grinding teeth are peculiarly adapted to the mastication of grass. Its usual habitat is hill country where it has been found at elevations as high as 7,000 ft. above sea level.

THE SUMATRAN TWO-HORNED RHINOCEROS (*RHINOCEROS SUMATRENSIS* CUV.).

The Sumatran Rhinoceros differs from the two other Asiatic Rhinoceroses in possessing two horns. On this account it is considered to represent a distinct sub-generic group (*Diocerhinus*). It is further distinguished by having a single pair of lower front teeth instead of two pairs as in the Indian and Javan animals.

The Two-horned Rhinoceros, like the Lesser One-horned species has a preference for forested hill tracts where it wanders up to considerable elevations. A sufficiency of shade and a good supply of water are essential to its habitat. A pair will frequent a given area for a time and then move off, their movements being affected by the water supply. They enter streams by night and also during the hot hours of the day. In suitable spots there are regular wallows or 'mud baths' in which the huge creatures roll much as buffaloes and pigs do. As a result of this habit their bodies are always well coated with mud. Tracks lead off in all directions from these 'wallows'. They present the appearance of large tunnels hollowed through the dense undergrowth. Unlike the elephant, a rhinoceros does not break through the jungle but burrows his way through the dense tangle. They visit the wallows singly or a bull and a cow may be found together. The night and early morning is spent in wandering about and feeding; the hot hours of the day in rest in some cool and shaded spot. In the cold weather and rains they visit the low country coming down in search of particular foods. They are not grazers but browse on twigs, shoots and are very partial to fallen fruit:—wild mangoes, citrous fruits and figs.

The sense of smell and hearing is acute but the sight is poor. Collections of dung found at particular places reveal a habit similar to that noticed with the Great One-horned Rhinoceros.

Little is known about their breeding habits but it is known that the young remain with the mother to a fairly advanced age.

The Two-horned Rhinoceros was once fairly common throughout Burma—it also occurred in Assam from which province it is now practically exterminated. At the present time a few inhabit the forests of Lower Tenasserim and the hill tracts about Myitkyina, the Arrakan Hills and the Pegu Yomas. A small number are present in the Shive-u-daung Sanctuary in the Mogok division of the Katha District where proper protection may save this species from extinction in Burmese limits.

Family III: *TAPIRIDAE*: TAPIRS.

THE MALAY TAPIR (*TAPIRUS INDICUS* CUV.).

The third and least specialised family of surviving Odd-toed Ungulates contains a single genus—*Tapirus*, the Tapirs. Tapirs differ little in their anatomy from their fossil ancestors and appear to have retained their primitive character even to our times. In the remote past they probably inhabited, as they do now, the deep recesses of the forest. Such protected environment is never favourable to rapid evolution but rather to persistence of type. We see this exemplified in the Two-horned Rhinoceros, like the Tapir, a creature of dense forest which shows little change in its anatomy as compared with the Two-horned Rhinoceros of past geological epochs.

Tapirs differ from all odd-toed ungulates in having 4 toes on the front feet. Their hind feet as with the Rhinoceros is three-toed. The three large toes of the fore foot correspond to the three middle fingers of the human hand. The little outer toe represents the fifth finger.

The cheek teeth have two simple transverse crests on their crowns, very different from the complex enamel foldings of the teeth of rhinoceroses and horses.

A heavy ungainly body, short stout limbs, a muzzle lengthened to form a short trunk, small eyes, oval ears and stumpy tail, all give the Tapir a peculiarly antedeluvian appearance.

Tapirs once inhabited Europe and from thence they appear to have migrated southwards. One group reached the New World where they still survive in Central and South America and the other passed down into the Malay countries.

The Malay species is very distinct from its American relations. It is larger and has a bi-coloured coat. The head, limbs and front part of the body is brownish black, the rest of the body behind the shoulders is greyish white. The American Tapirs are uniform brown. The young of both animals are striped. The Malay Tapir stands from 3-3½ ft. at the withers and slightly higher at the rump. The species is confined to Sumatra and the Malay Peninsula and only enters our limits in the south of Tenasserim. Here it lives in densest forests and has many of the habits of the rhinoceros browsing on leaves and twigs and visiting wallows. It is a water loving creature and swims and dives well. A pair of Tapir in captivity displayed a habit of carefully concealing their droppings. Copulation took place in the water. A single young was produced. The period of gestation was 9 months.

PROBOSCIDEA: ELEPHANTS.

The proboscis or trunk of the elephant gives the name Proboscidea to this the fourth and last order of Ungulates. There are but two species of elephants in existence—the Indian and the African. They are the sole survivors of a great assemblage of species which once inhabited the earth. No fewer than seven species of elephants and 8 different Mastodons are known to have existed in India during remote geological periods.

With its pendant trunk, its curious dentition, and its great size the elephant presents distinctive characters which differentiate it from all other mammals. However remarkable these characters may be, they are the ultimate results of a gradual deviation from a standard type of mammal—a hairy creature of no great size walking on the soles of its five-toed feet and carrying in its jaws the typical complement and number of incisor, canine and molar teeth. A comparison of existing and extinct forms of elephants and their allies has helped to indicate the great physical changes which the race has undergone during the long ages of its history. Changes which have been brought about largely by migrations to new countries and the new condition of life which they imposed. These migrations were impelled not only by the natural urge of the creature to extend its territory but also by actual changes in the earth's surface which bringing about a difference in climate and vegetation forced the ancestral forms to migrate into areas where conditions of life were more congenial. The physical modifications which elephants display are seen firstly in an increase in size. This necessitated the development of pillar-like limbs to support the enormous weight of the body which again implied the straightening of the limb bones and a change in the angle of their articulation. The foot itself changed its posture from the primitive plantigrade position. The heel and ankle bones were elevated above the ground and a thick pad of gristle developed beneath each foot and so formed a cushion to receive its share of the weight. The toes were embedded in the common mass of the cylindrical foot and encased in a common skin. Their position is indicated externally by broad flat nails which may be fewer than the number of toes. Thus, the limb bones gradually developed into vertical shafts through which the weight of the body was transmitted.

The shortness of the neck and the height of the head from the ground necessitated the development of a proboscis or trunk—a combined and lengthened nose and upper lip—as a device for securing food and water. Its development was accompanied by marked changes in the character and form of the skull. The skull of an elephant shows no 'snout'. The bony part of the face is almost straight. But it would appear that the ancestral elephants had a longer face—a prolonged bony snout more in conformity with the standard mammal skull. This is seen to some extent in the skull of the American Mastodon and to a more remarkable degree in a yet more ancient form of Mastodon—the *Tetrabelodon*. The creature had an extraordinary lengthened lower jaw furnished with two horizontal tusks. These tusks were additional to a downward bent pair in the upper jaw. Its trunk must have rested horizontally on its lower jaw between the tusks. It was not a pendant trunk but an elongated upper lip. It is believed that an elephant's trunk originated in this way. Firstly by the great elongation of the lower jaw producing a corresponding lengthening of the proboscis to reach to the end of the tusks and then by a shrinkage of the lower jaw and the straightening of the bones of the face. The long proboscis was no longer supported by the lower jaw. Gradually dropping as the lower jaw receded, in the course of successive ages, it at last hung down as a pendant trunk.

Other physical changes undergone by elephants are seen in increase in the size and complexity of the teeth, their consequent diminution in number and the development of a peculiar method of tooth succession. All the canine teeth have been lost and all the incisors, except the second pair in the upper jaw. These have developed into tusks. As to the grinding teeth an elephant develops 6 molars in each jaw during its life time. But the jaws are so short and the grinders so large that there is never room for more than two—one entirely and the other partly exposed above the gums. The new tooth forms in the rear of the jaw. Pushing forward it gradually replaces the preceding tooth which, as it wears away, is crowded out of the jaw. The first milk molar appears at the age of two weeks, it is shed at the age of 2 years, the second is shed at the age of 6, the third at 9, the fourth (or first adult tooth) between the 20th and 25th year, the fifth at 60 and the sixth lasts for the remainder of the creature's life.

Each molar is larger than the one which preceded it. Its structure has no parallel in the teeth of other animals. It is made up of a series of plates each composed of a flattened mass of dentine invested by a layer of enamel, the whole bound together in a solid mass by cement. As the dentine wears the harder enamel appears in a series of transverse ridges across the crown of the molar. The number of these ridges varies. In the Indian elephant the last or 6th molar may show 27 of these ridges. In the African species the number never exceeds 11. The African elephant is larger than the Indian. It has enormous ears, a hollow back and only three nails on each hind foot. There are 4 in the Indian species. The trunk ends in two equal sized 'lips'. The Indian elephant has but one.

The *Proboscidea* form a single family the *Elephantidae* which includes but one living genus.

THE INDIAN ELEPHANT (*ELEPHAS MAXIMUS INDICUS*).

The Indian elephant rarely exceed 10 ft. 6 in. at the shoulder. The average height of an adult male is 9 ft. The female is a foot lower. Twice the circumference of an elephant's fore foot gives a fair indication of its height. The rule does not apply always in the case of young and growing animals.

Generally only the males have large tusks. The tusks of females scarcely protrude or perhaps protrude a few inches. In some males the tusks are no longer than in females. Many of these tuskless males or *maknas* are very large in build with extraordinarily well developed trunks. The contour of the tusks varies. In some elephants they are wide spread and curved, in others straight and pointed downwards. A pair in the Royal Museum at Siam taped 9 ft. 10½ in. A pair in the possession of H.M. the King measures 8 ft. 9 in. and 8 ft. 6½ in. and weighs 160 and 161 lbs. respectively. The elephants found in Ceylon are regarded as a separate race (*E. maximus zeylanicus*). The males carry quite normal tusks. The females are tuskless. A few big tuskers shot in Ceylon are believed to be the descendants of elephants introduced from India.

The Indian Elephant has normally five nails on its fore foot and four on its hind. The outside nails are comparatively small and crinkled and their impression is only traceable in very wet soil. Ordinarily the imprint of at most three nails is to be seen and that only on soft ground. The colour of the elephant is greyish black. The chest, forehead and ears are often covered with flesh coloured spots.

An elephant usually moves at a walking pace, when alarmed or annoyed it breaks into a shuffling run. The huge creature can attain a wonderful speed and when 'all out' may travel at quite 20 miles an hour. Despite its bulk the elephant is wonderfully active going up and down steep hill sides with ease. It is an excellent swimmer and in deep water swims with practically the whole body except part of the head and trunk submerged.

Elephants chiefly frequent districts covered with tall forests where the ground is hilly or undulating and where bamboos grow in profusion. They are extremely adaptable and will live in steamy humid jungle or in cool elevated forests. In Burma they wander at all seasons of the year into bamboo forest at a height of 10,000 ft. while in Sikkim, their tracks have been seen in the snow 12,000 ft. above sea level. In the dry season the herds generally keep to the denser forests but during the rains come out into open glades and frequently enter cultivation. Individuals of various sizes and ages associate in herds which may vary from 5 to 60 or more animals. Herds are believed to be composed of single families. Different herds do not mix but stray females and young males may migrate from one herd into another. When fodder is scarce, the larger herds break up into small parties, which reunite when conditions are favourable. The big tuskers are usually seen feeding at some distance from the main herd. The bulls when they arrive at a certain age, live as solitaries or, two males of equal age may associate together. A solitary bull will graze with a herd when it happens to be in the same patch of jungle and will seek the herd when the urge to mate is on it and desert it again when its desire is appeased. When travelling elephants move in single file, the tuskers generally bringing up the rear. The leader of a herd is invariably an old female. Herds travel to and from their feeding grounds by well worn paths, wandering from them when the terrain is favourable but returning to these fixed paths, which generally follow the easiest and straightest line across the country and represent the accumulated wisdom of generations of travelling elephants. When undisturbed, the herd pursues a regular and ordered routine, drinking and feeding in accustomed places and lying up to rest in its usual retreat. They sleep during the hot hours of the day, being intolerant of the sun, feed early in the morning and evening and come out after nightfall to feed in open forest or to raid crops; retiring to sleep after midnight. An elephant rests standing or stretched out on its side. The food consists of various kinds of grasses and leaves, stems and leaves of wild bamboos and plantains, all species of crops and the bark of particular kinds of trees. A full grown elephant will eat from 600-700 lbs. of green fodder in a day.

Male elephants, very rarely females, both tame and wild, on attaining maturity are subject to peculiar periodical paroxysms of excitement known as '*musth*'. *Musth* seems to have some connection with the sexual functions. It is probably analogous to the 'rut' in deer. It occurs most frequently during the cold season and may perhaps be due to ungratified sexual desire. In some cases this is not always so since the society of a female will by no means quell or pacify the animal. At other times an elephant in musth will seek a mate.

The exact breeding season is uncertain but as most of the young are dropped in the late autumn and the period of gestation lasts about 20 months it is probable that the main breeding season is during the hot weather and at the commencement of the rains. One calf is only born at a time though, in rare instances twins and once, even triplets have been recorded. The mother of a young calf is invariably assisted in caring for her young by another female who takes on the duties of a guardian and is as assiduous in her care of the calf as its parent. A new born calf will walk a few hours after birth. In height it averages about 2 ft. 10 in. It suckles with its mouth and when alarmed takes refuge under its mother's body.

Elephants have a very poor sight, the sense of smell and hearing is highly developed, more so than in most animals. Much mystery is attached to the deaths of elephants. They are reputed to seek out some solitary and secluded spot to which they retreat when they feel their powers failing and death approaching. The legend is widespread, though it remains to be substantiated. The fact that dead elephants are seldom found may be explained firstly by the infrequency with which deaths must occur among such long lived animals and secondly by the rapidity with which decomposition in a tropical climate will remove all traces of the carcase. There are some instances on record where other elephants have attempted to move or have actually moved the dead body of a companion.

CARNIVORA OR BEASTS OF PREY.

The Carnivora or flesh-eaters is a name given to a distinctive group of animals known familiarly as 'Beasts of Prey'. The assemblage includes the cats, great and small, and such varied animals as civets, dogs, bears and the weasels and their numerous kindred. It also includes the aquatic beasts of prey—seals, sea-lions and walruses.

Not all these animals are exclusively or even mainly flesh-eaters. Some live partly on vegetable food. Again, many mammals not classed as carnivores feed on flesh. The Australian Dassyures, creatures not much bigger than a cat with the predaceous habits of weasels are wholly carnivorous. But they, like the well-known kangaroo, are broadly distinguished as Marsupials or 'pouched' animals. With this exception it might be said that there is no group of mammals which feeds so generally on flesh.

The Carnivora as a whole reveal in their structure certain characters which are common to all of them and which mark them as animals whose particular role is the capture and destruction of living prey. The evidence of a predatory life is most signally revealed in the structure of their teeth and claws—essential weapons designed to secure for the beast of prey its appropriate food. Very striking in the skull of a carnivore are the canine teeth. The majority of mammals have canine teeth, but in carnivores the canines tend to become larger and stronger than the incisors and in some of the great cats these teeth are represented by enormous offensive fangs. Their special purpose is the seizing and holding of prey. All carnivores have 6 incisors. Usually, the outer incisor in the upper jaw is the largest and sometimes it is so large and pointed that it looks like a small canine. Canines and incisors provide the beast of prey with appropriate weapons for seizing, holding and biting. The mastication of food is the work of the cheek or molar teeth. Among carnivores there is much variation in form and structure of the molar teeth—variation which is related to some extent to the degree to which a particular animal is or is not wholly carnivorous.

Apart from the teeth, the most distinctive feature in the skull of a carnivore is the mode of articulation of the lower jaw. It is connected to the skull and moves on a small transverse hinge. The device gives strength to the joint but deprives the animal of the power of moving its jaws from side to side or backwards and forwards. Movement is limited to an up and down biting or snapping action, and the grip of the jaws is intensified by the great biting muscles which secure the lower jaw to the skull. Strong cheek arches and ridges have been developed in the skull to provide an attachment for these muscles.

All the carnivores have never less than four toes on each foot and these are generally armed with strong sharp claws. The clavicle or collar bone is frequently absent in beasts of prey. This is a feature which they share with hoofed animals. When present, it never forms a complete connection between the breast bone and the shoulder blade. It is reduced to a splint of bone embedded in the muscles of the chest. The brain of a carnivore is well developed and the stomach is always simple.

These are some of the characters which distinguish carnivores from other mammals.

In themselves they form a varied assemblage in which two great divisions are recognised. One includes the terrestrial and the other the aquatic Beasts of Prey.

Seals, walruses and sea-lions form the latter group. Descendants of land-dwelling carnivores, as a result of subsequent development into animals whose element is the water, they have undergone many changes in form and structure and have lost some of the main features which distinguish their terrestrial relatives. The name *Pinnipedia* or 'fin-footed', by which this sub-division of the Carnivores is known, describes the condition of their hands and feet which have been modified into flippers. Mainly inhabitants of cold seas, none of these animals is found in India.

The terrestrial Beasts of Prey are called *Fissipedia* or 'free-footed', in allusion to their distinct and separate toes which are never encased in skin to form a fin or flipper.

As organs of locomotion the limbs are not swimming but essentially walking, running or climbing organs. Walking is effected either on the entire sole of the foot as in the bears or, as in cats and dogs, mainly upon the toes with the hinder part of the foot held clear from the ground. A somewhat intermediate mode of walking is found among weasels, otters and badgers. Most carnivores are good climbers. Some live almost entirely in trees.

Terrestrial beasts of prey display a varied and highly developed armament of teeth. While the canine and incisor teeth of various species are on the whole tolerably uniform, the molar or cheek teeth display numerous and interesting variations. A reduction in the number of cheek teeth and the compression of their crowns into narrow cutting edges generally indicate an exclusive diet of flesh. While the more numerous the cheek teeth and the broader their crowns, the more likely it is that the owner subsists on a mixed diet. Extremes of these two types are seen in the cats and the bears—one wholly carnivorous the other mainly herbivorous; while stages between the two may be traced through other forms of Carnivora. A striking peculiarity in the molar teeth of beasts of prey is the development of a carnassial or 'flesh-tooth'. In the majority of families it is larger than the other cheek teeth. The flesh tooth in the upper jaw is always the last premolar—its antagonist in the lower jaw is the first true molar. The crown of the upper flesh tooth consists of two parts, a sharp edged blade divided by notches into two or more cusps borne upon two inner roots and the 'tubercle' a short blunt cusp supported by a separate root. In carnivores which are purely flesh feeders—the flesh tooth is conspicuous—its blade well developed and its 'tubercle' reduced in size. An increase in the tubercular character of the tooth is usually traceable through those genera which are mixed feeders. In bears, the flesh tooth is scarcely distinguishable from the other cheek teeth. The lower flesh tooth varies in form. In cats, its crown consists solely of a blade which is divided into two large pointed cusps. Behind these cusps there is a small rudimentary third division. The opposing blades of the upper and lower flesh teeth work against one another with a scissor-like action. They provide the mechanism for shearing flesh from bones or crushing hard food. Generally the molars in front of the flesh tooth are sharp pointed and compressed, those behind are broad and tuberculated.

With the exception of Australia and New Zealand, the Carnivora inhabit all the countries and larger islands of the Globe from the icy oceans of the Arctic Circle to the tropical plains of India and Africa. Some, like cats and dogs, have a world-wide distribution; others, like the hyaenas and civets, are restricted in their range. In the earliest part of the Tertiary epoch there were numerous Carnivores small and large. Their skulls were much like those of existing Carnivora. They had cutting teeth and clawed feet. The brain was small. They are now grouped in a distinct sub-order—the *Creodonta.* Some of them were the ancestors of modern Carnivores. Others have left no descendants. In habit and general appearance these primitive carnivores were like the modern beasts of prey—but the various distinctive features of the modern races are found in these ancient forms in different combinations.

Various carnivores related to the modern forms lived during the latter part of the Tertiary period. Perhaps the largest of them were the Amphicyons. Classed among the dogs, the amphicyon equalled the biggest bear in size and revealed in its structure some affinity to these animals. A survivor of this archaic animal lived in the Siwaliks. These mountains were also the home of two species of sabre-toothed tigers (*Machærodus*) representatives of a family of extinct cats. The sabre-toothed tiger had enormous upper canines. They took the form of great slightly curved compressed fangs with serrated edges. The jaws were loose hung and could be opened wide enough to allow full play for the action of the tusks and so allow the powerful muscles at the back of the neck to drive them down vigorously into the body of an enemy.

The modern land Carnivora are divided into three sections, the distinctive characters between them being derived mainly from difference in the structure of the base of the skull. These sections are: (1) the *Aeluroidea* or Cat Section; (2) *Cynoidea* or Dog Section; and (3) the *Arctoidea* or Bear Section. Each of these three animals the cat, the dog and the bear provides the pattern of its group.

The Cat group or *Æluroidea* includes the cats, civets, mongooses and hyaenas. The Dog group, *Cynoidea*: dogs, jackals, wolves and foxes. The Bear group, *Arctoidea*: bears, badgers, racoons, martins and weasels.

ÆLUROIDEA: Cat Section.

Family I. *FELIDAE*: CATS.

The Cats, great and small, though they vary much in size and habits, form a well-marked tribe with characters which distinguish them from all other Carnivores. Splendidly equipped for their role in life, they represent the Beast of Prey in its perfection. The Cats are supreme in armament of tooth and claw, in their combination of grace, strength and agility.

None of the Beasts of Prey display so powerful a development of teeth as some of the great cats and in none are the teeth so perfectly adapted to a purely carnivorous diet. Increased sturdiness and strength has been attained in their jaw bones by a reduction in their length. The comparative shortness of the jaws in relation to the length of the head gives the Cats that flatness of feature which contrasts so markedly with the pointed muzzles of civets or the long snouts of dogs and bears.

With the shortening of the jaw bones there has been a corresponding loss in the number of cheek teeth. Cats have much fewer cheek teeth than dogs or other more generalised forms of carnivores. Speaking generally, an exclusive diet of flesh is indicated by a level row of small pincer-like incisors, by large, deeply implanted and widely separated canines and lastly by a reduction in the number of molar teeth—the normally broad grinding crowns of those that remain being compressed into sharp-edged cutting implements.

This is a condition seen in its most perfect form in the teeth of cats. A modification in the number and shape of their teeth has been effected in early stages of their evolution by those processes which adapt the structure of a creature to its specific needs. A study of the teeth of primitive and now extinct forms of cats shows that the perfecting of their dental armament has been arrived at by stages. Firstly there was a reduction in the number of cheek teeth, followed by an enlargement of the canines which took their conical form and finally came the modification of the cheek teeth into purely cutting instruments.

In existing cats the first cheek tooth in the upper jaw is small or sometimes absent. The second cheek tooth shows a sudden increase in size. It is a large and sharply bladed tooth. The third tooth displays even greater gain in strength and size. Its crown is divided by two notches into 3 sharp pointed blades. This is the upper carnassial or 'flesh tooth'. It is the last premolar in the upper jaw. Tucked away behind this great tooth and set transversely to it is the solitary surviving molar. From its size and position it can be of little significance in mastication.

Of the three cheek teeth in the lower jaw the first two are premolars, and third and last tooth is a true molar. It is divided by a V-shaped notch into two blades. It functions as the lower 'flesh tooth'. The peculiar articulation of the lower jaw to the skull which is characteristic in beasts of prey prevents a circular grinding action and confines the play of the cheek teeth to a vertical up and down movement in which their compressed and sharp edged crowns working against one another cut and coarsely divide the flesh. The deep rooted trenchant and sharp pointed canine teeth are well adapted to hold, to pierce and lacerate struggling prey. We have referred to the reduction in size or complete suppression of the first cheek tooth. This leaves a space between the molars and canines. Thus, the great canines which interlock in the closed jaw stand clear when the jaws open and are driven full into the flesh of a victim. There are no contiguous teeth to obstruct their complete penetration.

There is a level row of 6 small pincer shaped incisors in the upper and lower jaw. Their purpose is to gnaw the soft gristly ends of bones and scrape off the tendinous attachments of the muscles. The array of sharp incisors, the powerful canines, the blade-like molars, have their special function and each is perfect for its special purpose. This armament of teeth supported on short powerful jaws controlled by great biting muscles, for whose attachment special provision has been made in the wide sturdy cheek arches and the bony crest of the skull, complete the Cat's formidable equipment for the killing and ingestion of its prey.

But carnivorous animals which tear to pieces and swallow their food can scarcely derive much enjoyment from its taste. It is only in Man and those herbivorous animals which prepare their food by mastication that the sense exhibits much delicacy of perception and the tongue attains a perfect adaptation to this end. In the Cats the mechanical function of the tongue predominates over the sensitive. Numerous papillae which cover the tongues of animals make them rough to the touch. In cats this roughness is greatest. These lingual papillae are of three types. In the Cats those which function as organs of taste are reduced to small dimensions. They are scattered about the surface of the tongue and are more abundant on its margins. Most numerous and prominent are the 'conical papillae'. In cats these conical papillae are encased in horny, pointed sheaths which stick into one's fingers like so many pins. Their function is purely mechanical. Their numerous sharp and rigid points give the tongue the action of a rasp. Bones are not usually crushed and swallowed by cats. They are licked clean and left and the rasp-like tongue is well adapted to remove the remnants of flesh which adhere to a bone. In the Cats the conical papillae tend to form a 'spiny patch' on the fore-part of the tongue which is surrounded by a zone of smaller papillae. The proximity of or the distance of this spinous patch from the apex of the tongue, its extent, the shape of the spines which form the cluster, are distinctive in certain groups of cats. A study of the lingual papillae in the Felidae, their character and arrangement has offered a means of throwing fresh light on the relationship of the different species.

Like the teeth, the strongly curved claws of cats reveal a perfection of development unequalled by other carnivores.

A beautiful and peculiar provision is seen in the structure of the foot whereby the claws are kept constantly sharp and are never worn down by contact with the ground. The terminal or claw bearing joint is so articulated that in its normal position it lies folded back on or against the preceding joint. In this reverted, partly erect position the claw at its summit is raised off the ground. An elastic ligament holds the joint erect and the claw is received into a sheath of skin specially devised for its reception. When the animal springs upon or strikes at its prey, a tendon clamped to the undersurface of the terminal joint and connected to the great flexor muscles of the limb pulls upon this joint and draws it from its reverted position downwards and forwards. The claws emerge from their sheaths and are bared for action.

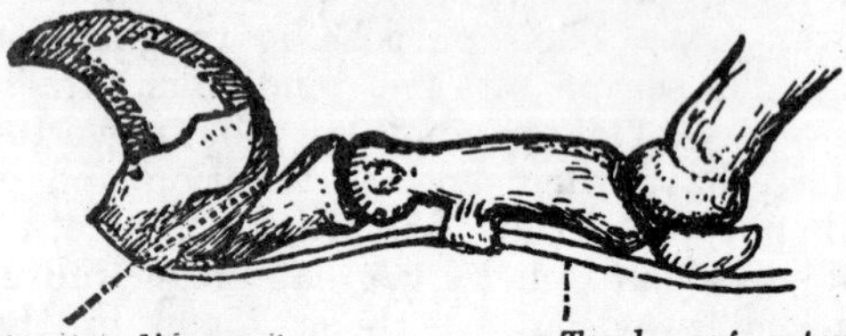

A. *Retractor ligament.* *Tendon of extensor muscle.*

B. *Retractor ligament.* *Tendon of extensor muscle.*

Bones and tendons of toe of the Cat. A, claw retracted and held erect by retractor ligament. B, claw extended, pulled downwards and forwards by extensor tendon.

How far the sheaths protect the claws depends upon two factors, the extent to which the claw-bearing joint can be drawn backwards and the length of the sheaths themselves. The Cheetah or Hunting Leopard is often described as having imperfectly retractile claws. A cheetah has the mechanism for retracting its claws and can draw them back as well as some species of cats, but the constantly bared condition of its claws is due to the rudimentary condition of the claw sheaths. These claw sheaths are by no means equally developed in all the Cats. In their most elaborate form as seen in the Lynx, the Tiger or the Leopard, the pollex or thumb is enveloped in a hood-like sheath and the lobes of the sheaths protecting the other claws are large enough to completely enfold them. In some of the smaller cats on the other hand the lobes of the sheath are not equally developed on all the digits and some of the claws are not completely covered—a condition not far removed from that of the civets. Between these two extremes every gradation in the development of the claw sheaths may be seen in cats.

Let us now consider movement in cats and their faculties of sight, scent and hearing—means by which they hunt their prey.

All cats are digitigrade. They walk on their toes and not upon the palms or soles of their feet. When walking the hinder part of the foot is entirely raised from the ground the weight of the body is taken by the toes—but not by the tips of the toes as in hoofed animals. This mode of progression is an improvement on the flat-footed gait of bears or of those carnivores which walk partly on their toes and partly on the soles of their feet. It makes for greater agility of movement.

A cat has five toes on its fore-foot and four on its hind. The innermost toe of the fore-foot, the pollex, corresponds to the thumb of the human hand. It is placed at a much higher level than the other toes and is of little use when walking. The missing toe in the hind-foot corresponds to the great toe of the human foot.

Soft pads under the toes and a broad cushion-like pad under the ends of the bones on which the foot rests when walking help the cat's stealthy movements. Its sinuous supple body, its muffled tread, its gliding progress, brought about by a simultaneous movement of the limbs on each side—concur in effecting a noiseless approach to its prey.

Cats have the largest eyes of all the carnivores. A well-developed system of muscles within the eye contracts the pupils in bright light and protects the eyes from glare and by dilating them in darkness allows as much light as possible to enter the eye and so improves its vision. The form taken by the contracting pupil differs markedly in the great and small cats. In domestic cats and in the smaller species generally, the pupil contracts to a narrow slit with two pinholes at each end through which alone the light enters. In the larger felines the contracting pupil takes a circular form.

It is generally agreed that when hunting the sense of smell is the dominant factor in dogs, in cats it is the sense of vision. It is suggested that the flat muzzle characteristic of cats leaves less space for the development of the nasal membranes which have greater scope for development in the longer muzzles of dogs, wolves and foxes. The relative development of the faculties of sight and scent appears to differ in various species of cats. The consensus of opinion is that the Tiger and the Panther display great acuteness of vision and, unlike the Lion, a corresponding dullness in their sense of smell. It is frequently held that these two animals depend mainly on sight and hearing when hunting. But it is difficult to conceive that animals which hunt under cover of darkness do not make the fullest use of both the faculties of sight and scent when seeking their prey, particularly in forest where vision may be circumscribed. At present we have only the vaguest knowledge as to how far purely nocturnal animals depend on vision for obtaining their food. This is one of the reasons why it is so difficult to arrive at any definite conclusion as to the real value of 'concealing' colours in nocturnal animals.

It is believed that a pattern of spots and stripes—so common in the colouration of the cats—is protective. The variegation of tone breaks up the mass of the body, obscures its contours and so helps to conceal it. This is a common explanation of the purpose of markings in tigers, leopards and other beasts of prey. But a patterned hide, if useful to the hunter, would be equally useful to its quarry. Many species of deer which are the accustomed prey of great cats are uniformly coloured when adult, whereas a concealing pattern on their coats would have proved a useful factor in evading detection. Now, if a spotted condition of the young is taken to indicate the primitive colouring of the parents, then the majority of deer are descendants of striped or banded ancestors and pattern in these animals has since been discarded—at least in the colouring of the adults of most species. This suggests that in these animals its significance as a factor in the struggle for existence could have been of no great importance.

Again, the absence of stripes and spots in the lion and other carnivores places them at no disadvantage in securing their prey. Like the tiger, the lion hunts in shadowy forest, in open bush or in grassland and it is claimed that in the African reed beds—a favourite hunting ground of lions—a vertically striped coat would have provided an ideal concealing pattern.

While a variegated colouration may prove a factor in the protection of lesser and more sedentary creatures; it cannot be regarded as essential to the equipment of a beast of prey. Cats, great and small, owe their ascendancy to their perfect mastery over the craft of hunting. Strong and active, of high intelligence, they display a perfection of senses and bodily organism which gives them mastery over creatures in which a ceaseless struggle for existence has perfected the means of escape.

As with all animals the ground colour of the cats varies with environment. There is the change from the light drab tones of desert species to the rich dark colouration of those living in more humid forests. The law of assimilation of colour to environment is more or less constant in Nature. Hazardous deductions of its purpose may lead us into beliefs which are at variance with evidence revealed by the actual lives and habits of animals.

The pattern of different species of cats is in general constant. Individual variations occur. Stripes sometimes break up into spots and spots show a tendency to run into stripes but as a general rule each species breeds true to its local type and there is little change in pattern except perhaps in its accentuation, lightening or obliteration with age. The lion and the puma are uniformly coloured when adult, though spotted or striped when cubs, which is taken as an indication of their descent from striped or spotted ancestors. There is a theory that there have been definite stages in the evolution of stripes and spots in the Felidae. The theory assumes that in the primitive condition, the stripes were longitudinal—a condition now common in the civets—next of kin to the cats. In the second stage the longitudinal stripes broke up into spots. Many civets and some cats again exhibit this pattern. It is perhaps also illustrated in the pattern of the Spotted Deer—the linear arrangement of the spots on its lower flanks suggests longitudinal stripes which have broken up into spots. In the third stage the spots reformed into vertical stripes such as one sees in the tiger, in the banded civet and in certain antelopes. The patternless hide of the adult lion or the puma is taken as the culminating phase in the evolution of markings. If this theory is correct then the progenitors of the tiger were longitudinally banded animals whose descendants passed through a spotted stage and finally attained the transverse stripes of existing tigers. The oblique direction of the stripes on the hind quarters and other parts of the tiger's body, the curious variations in their markings where spots crop up between stripes or stripes tend to continue as faint spots or to double up into loops or the rudiments of a 'rosette' are taken to lend support to this theory. Again the curious variations sometimes exhibited by lion cubs in which spots show a tendency to fuse into stripes, are also quoted as supporting evidence.

To sum up the distinctive characters of Cats as a tribe. There is the shortening of the muzzle—the reduction in the number of cheek teeth, the powerful development of the canines and flesh teeth, the strongly curved retractile claws. These are characters which mark them as a natural and distinctive group of animals. But it has been the contention of zoologists during the last half century that the comprehensive genus *Felis* in which all cats great and small were included required regrouping into several distinct genera. Various attempts to do this have been made by naturalists. The most recent is by Pocock. His purpose was to indicate more clearly the true relationship of different forms of cats and to dispose of such fictitious groupings as imply a close relationship between the Lion and the Puma or give an erroneous impression of the relative affinities of such creatures as the tiger, the domestic cat and the lynx. He based his classification on the variations which are apparent in the structure of the hyoid apparatus in different forms of cats, on differences in the form of the feet and the cutaneous sheaths guarding the claws. He divides the family Felidae into three well-marked groups:

(i) The *Pantherinae* which comprises the Lion, the Tiger, the Panther, the Jaguar and the Ounce.
(ii) The *Acinonychinae* the Cheetahs or Hunting-Leopards.
(iii) The *Felinae* which includes the Puma, the Lynx, and all the smaller cats.

As regards the scientific names of different species, many have received more than one name from naturalists and the tracing of the correct name from the tangle of zoological literature is a matter of no small difficulty. Here again we have followed the nomenclature adopted by Pocock in his recent papers on Felidae which include a careful revision of the synonymy of the various species with which they deal.

With the exception of the Australian continent and Madagascar—the range of cats is universal—the headquarters of the tribe is the Old World. Sixteen different species occur in India and its dependencies, a larger concentration than is to be found in any tract of similar size on the Earth's surface. Of the cats living within our borders during past geological epochs, more than 7 species are known, some similar to existing forms others now extinct. Among them was *Felis cristata* which was quite as large as the tiger and two extinct species of sabre-toothed tigers (*Machærodus*) one peculiar to India.

Sub-family: I. *PANTHERINAE.*

The Lion, Tiger, Leopard, Jaguar and Ounce.

While most cats, particularly the larger species, are readily distinguished by their form, colour or size it is less simple to discover among them differences in anatomy which offer a clue to the true affinities which exist between the different members of the tribe—distinctions which would help us to discriminate between closely related forms and those which reveal a lesser degree of kinship. Perhaps the most striking variation in the internal anatomy of cats is to be found in the mode of attachment of the hyoid apparatus. It is perhaps an obscure detail in the structure of cats but the mode of attachment of the hyoid has an influence in some way on the voice of the animal—on the power and variety of tone it can produce. Now a similarity of voice is considered nearly always a good indication of affinity among animals. Resemblances or differences in the structure of the hyoid therefore provide evidence which is useful in the classification of the felines. In the lower Vertebrates, in fishes for example, the elaborate hyoid apparatus is importantly connected with the respiratory function, but in mammals it is reduced to a much simpler condition. The apparatus, usually composed of a number of small bones, is named *Hyoid* because of the arrangement these bones in the shape of an arch or of the Greek letter Y. In mammals the arms of the hyoid are suspended from the posterior part of the skull to provide a support for the root of the tongue and for the larynx i.e. the extended part of the wind pipe which contains the vocal chords. The apparatus comes away when the soft parts of the skull are removed. In the smaller cats arms of the hyoid are composed of an uninterrupted chain of small bones which hold the larynx close to the skull and so restrict its power of movement. In the great cats —in the lion, tiger, panther, jaguar and ounce—the arms of the hyoid are imperfectly ossified. In the lower part the small bones are replaced by elastic ligaments. In the lion these tendons may be 6 in. long and may stretch to 9 in. The elasticity given to the hyoid by these tendons allows greater mobility to the larynx. It is not drawn up close to the skull but is embedded in the mobile muscles of the throat. The difference in the mode of attachment of the hyoid seen in the great and smaller cats has resulted in those differences in voice which is so noticeable among them.

The lion, tiger, leopard and jaguar are able to roar but are incapable of purring; while the cheetah, the puma and the smaller cats, whose hyoid is differently constructed, do not roar but can express contentment by purring. Though the roars of the great felines are more or less distinguishable there is an underlying distinctiveness in the power and variety of sounds they produce which is due to the distinctive structure of the hyoid. It differentiates them from the other cats and offers an indication of their affinity to one another. Evidence of relationship between the great felines is also traced in a similarity of pattern in the cubs which may be taken as a specific character. The lion shows a pattern intermediate between the tiger and the leopard and the leopard in its markings shows a definite affinity to the jaguar. The ounce because of similarity in the structure of the hyoid is likewise included in this group of cats. The affinity between these animals is also indicated in a similarity in the position, extent and nature of the conical papillae which form the 'spinous' patch on the surface of the tongue, to which reference has already been made. In the great cats the patch commences near the apex but does not extend to the middle of the tongue. It is a condition which does not occur in the tongues of other cats and provides further evidence of structural kinship between these great felines.

THE ASIATIC LION (*PANTHERA LEO PERSICA* MEYER).

The racial name *persica* is given to lions found in India, Persia or Mesopotamia One species of lion inhabits both Africa and Asia, but minor differences, more or less constant, are considered sufficient to indicate a racial distinction between Asiatic and African lions. These distinctions do not always hold when individuals from the two countries are compared. They can only be regarded as average differences.

On the average, the Indian lion has a scantier mane than the African and, curiously enough, in combination with this character a fuller coat, a longer tassel of hair at the end of the tail, a more pronounced tuft of hair on the elbow joints and a fuller fringe of hairs on the belly. In size, there is little to choose between the two. The average length of African and Asiatic lions is a few inches over 9 ft. The largest recorded measurement of an Indian lion is 9 ft. 7 in., of an African lion 10 ft. 7 in.

The colour of the lion is tawny. The density of the tone varies in different individuals. Some lions are deep yellowish brown, others are pale, in others again the prevalent tone is sandy grey. Dark tips to the hairs may give the coat a finely mottled effect.

The cubs are spotted and striped. The pattern is taken to indicate descent from a progenitor with markings midway between the spots of a leopard and the stripes of a tiger. The markings fade with growth though an indication of them may be seen in well-grown animals. The colour of the mane may differ little from the tawny tint of the body or it may be more or less sharply differentiated by a lesser or greater intermingling of brown or black hairs. A predominance of black hairs in the mane gives rise to the term 'black maned' lions. Both light and dark maned lions with intergradations between the two may be seen in India though 'black' manes are rare. The mane of the lion begins to grow at 3 years and is said to be complete in about 6 years.

Fully and poorly maned lions are found in India as in Africa. Luxuriance or scantiness of mane is probably an individual character; some animals being more hairy than others. The average scantiness of mane seen in the Indian lion is certainly not due to the mane being 'combed' out in the thorny forests in which these animals live in this country.

The Gir Forest, lying within Junagadh State covers nearly 500 square miles of rugged undulating country. It is composed mainly of stunted teak trees, palas, jambul, babul and bhor, and patches of small bamboo with an undergrowth of thorny shrubs and bushes.

This is the nature of the only forest in which lions are now found in India. Their movements within this forest are governed by the movements of the animals which they hunt—cattle, antelope and deer.

The Gir is bare and open during the hot weather. Its water supply over miles of arid country is limited to a few deep pools in the dry bed of the Hiran 'river' and in some of the nullahs, in the vicinity of which game and herds of grazing cattle concentrate. But in the rains, when the forest is overrun with rank grass and vegetation, abundance of grazing and an abundance of fresh water in its numerous nullahs results in a wider dispersal of animal life. Cattle graze outside forest limits. The lions following their prey, stray into the neighbouring lands.

Indian lions have much the same habits as African. They rest by day under cover. In the Gir they frequently lie up under the shade of some wide spreading banyan tree. At dusk they come out in quest for food. Their roars are heard through the night more noticeably at dusk and again just before daybreak.

Lions are said to rely mainly on scent and hearing when hunting. When hunting alone, a lion will stalk its prey or lie in ambush within 20 or 30 yards of the quarry, waiting to rush upon and seize it as it strays within reach. But when a troop of lions is hunting together, as frequently happens when there are family parties with half-grown young, a combination of effort has been observed among them. Some of the troop, keeping in touch with each other by low grunts, drive the distracted prey in the direction of others who lying silent intercept and slay the quarry. It is said, that in these combined hunts, it is the lion who drives the game and the lioness which kills it; half-grown cubs when present helping. The same combination in hunting has been observed occasionally in family parties of tigers.

Many observers have written about the social life of lions in Africa. How far these observations apply to the social life of lions in the Gir remains to be discovered. The paucity of numbers, the peculiar conditions under which lions live in the Gir may affect their social behaviour. The underlying cause of animals herding and remaining together is the reproductive instinct: care of the young by the parents prolongs the association. There are some who hold that the lion is a polygamist and that at mating time he acquires a following of females by right of conquest. Single lions with an attendant troop of females are frequently seen but it has also been observed that a lion will leave the troop and go off to live in seclusion with a mate.

There appears to be no particular breeding season. In the Gir the majority of lions appear to mate between October and November and the young are born generally between January and February. Cubs born during the wet season are less liable to survive—conditions in the forest are unfavourable to them and food is scarce. The lioness has her first litter when she is about 2½-3 years old. The period of gestation is 108 days. In the Gir forest the ordinary litter numbers two, frequently three. In the wild state the young are produced at intervals of at least 18 months to two years. The milk canines of a lion cub are not replaced by the permanent teeth till it is about a year old and up to that age the young lion is said to be comparatively helpless in fending for itself. First sharing in their 'kills', with growth the young lions improve their prentice efforts at killing and finally attain mastery in their craft. A number of lionesses with young may associate to form large troops. This herding of females and young is not an unusual feature among social animals. Among lions it probably simplifies the problem of food supply. Equally common is the forming of societies of young males. Young lions when able to fend for themselves may band together. They in turn join up with young lionesses and so form the nucleus of fresh troops. Old lions passed the capacity to hold their own against rivals lead solitary lives.

Within historic times the lion inhabited Northern Greece and Macedonia. Its range extended through Persia and Mesopotamia into the plains of Northern and Central India. Lions may still survive in the wilder parts of Persia and in Mesopotamia; in India they are found only within the province of Kathiawar and there only in the Gir Forest.

Man, the agent who exterminated the lion in Europe and other parts of Asia, was probably mainly responsible for bringing it to the verge of extinction in India. Even in parts of Africa lions are steadily retreating before European settlement. The bolder, more confiding habits of the lion, its herding instincts, the open nature of the country in which it lives provided the opportunity for its destruction in India and elsewhere. Even in the Province of Kathiawar, where tigers do not exist and where no struggle for supremacy between these two giants of the tribe could have taken place, the lion was slowly driven from the Barda and Aleche hills, from parts of Dhrangadra and Jasdan as a result of human settlement and the progress of cultivation.

The number of lions in the Gir is computed to be well below a hundred. It is feared that the small stock will deteriorate through inter-breeding. The laudable efforts of the Junagadh Durbar have so far saved this animal from complete extermination in India, but under existing circumstances it is essential that the neighbouring States should co-operate by refraining where possible from shooting such lions as stray into their borders.

THE TIGER (*PANTHERA TIGRIS* LINN.).

Like the human, the animal population of India has its foreign element. Our wild animals include many species which have migrated into India from countries far beyond our frontiers. Prominent among these is the tiger. Though intimately associated with India—the home of the tiger—the country of its origin is believed to be Central and Northern Asia.

Animals which have originated in a particular country have spread over and colonised great portions of the Earth's surface. The country of their origin is traced sometimes by the location of their fossil remains. The earliest known remains of the tiger—indistinguishable from those now living, were discovered in the New Siberian Islands well within the Arctic Circle. Time was, when under a genial climate, Northern and Central Asia supported a rich vegetation and a varied and abundant animal life. Fossil remains of animals discovered in this now bleak and desolate region reveal the past existence of a great variety of animals. Among them were reindeer and red deer, elk, bison and antelopes which, in their day, were preyed upon by tigers, lions and other carnivores.

From Northern Asia, the Tiger extended its territory over the greater part of the Continent, establishing itself wherever conditions were favourable. It did not colonise the high tableland of Tibet, where a combination of desert and arctic conditions prevail, nor did it enter the great Palaearctic Desert which stretches from the confines of Sind and Baluchistan through the greater part of Persia, Mesopotamia and Arabia. The most westerly limits of its migration appears to be the eastern slopes of the Caucasus, the forests of the Elburz Mountains, which lie between the shores of the Caspian and Persia and the northern frontiers of Afghanistan. It is still found in these regions. From the Persian border —its territory must have extended, or may still extend, through Turkestan into Northern Asia. Today, the Tiger survives in Amurland and Korea, in Eastern Siberia and in Mongolia and Manchuria. Southwards, its range extends through China into Burma, Siam and the Malay countries reaching its most southerly limits in the islands of Java, Sumatra and Bali. We are unable to conjecture how long ago the Tiger entered and established itself in India. Its absence from Ceylon suggests its arrival at the most southerly point of its distribution in this country after the land-bridge between India and Ceylon had disappeared. It was prevented from colonising the island by the deep intervening seas. That the Tiger was established in India fifty centuries ago is again suggested by the recent excavations at Mohenjodaro, where the records of a pre-Aryan civilization. whih flourished 5,000 years ago include numerous seals engraved with figures of the tiger.

The Tiger apparently entered India through the hill ranges of Assam. It colonised the thickly forested southern slopes of the Himalayas and subsequently established itself over the greater part of the Peninsula, avoiding its treeless and desert portions.

Variation in Tigers.

It will be seen that the tiger, unlike the lion, is exclusively an Asiatic animal. Throughout Asia there is but one species. Pocock recently summarised the external difference of tigers in different Asiatic countries. He considers that it is possible to distinguish eight races. The Indian Tiger (*Panthera tigris tigris*) is accepted as the typical tiger—a standard for comparison with the tigers of other countries. It is described as a rich coloured, well-striped animal with a short coat. The Caucasian Tiger is distinguished by a tendency to brown both in body colour and stripes. More or less distinct races are said to inhabit Mongolia, Manchuria and Amurland, Northern and Central China, Sumatra, Java and Bali. But series of skins and skulls from all the countries where tigers are found are required for comparison before we can arrive at definite conclusions as regards the extent of variation between the various races. Little is known even about the Indian Tiger. We have still to learn whether the tiger varies in different provinces in India and what differences in its colouration are produced by season or age. Individual variation is great.

Though tigers living in the more humid forests are generally darker and richer in colouring, pale and dark animals may be found in the same forest tract. Again the number of body stripes appears to have little relation to the part of the country in which the animal lives. The number varies in the same district. Some of the characters which distinguish different genera or distantly allied species of animals may have an adaptive significance. But the trivial differences seen in what we describe as sub-species, varieties or geographical races of an animal may have no adaptive importance in its mode of life and little adaptive relationship to the environment in which it lives.

Tigers in Northern Asia assume a heavy winter coat which is shed during the spring. Indian tigers go through a similar though less striking change. They moult their finer winter coats on the approach of the hot weather: the moult is at its height in March.

Size of Tigers.

Opinions differ as to whether the Indian Tiger equals the tigers of Northern Asia in build. Sportsmen in this country have argued about the size of tigers for well over a hundred years. Published records fluctuate between 9 and 14 ft. and some attain even more ambitious lengths. The varied methods used by sportsmen in measuring tigers would give widely different results if applied to the same animal. A stripped skin or a generous tape over curves yield remarkable, if inaccurate results. So might a man add to his height by taking in the contours of his body. A straight line measured between pegs driven at the extremities of the tiger's head and tail should be adopted as the standard to be followed by all sportsmen. It is preferable to register separate measurements of head and body, and the tail. A tiger measuring 10 ft. 7 in. on this basis would be a very large animal. Few Indian tigers exceed 10 ft. in length—the majority fall short of this limit.

The average length of a tiger is 9 ft. to 9 ft. 6 in. The average height 3 ft. to 3 ft. 6 in. The measurements of the skull may provide an index of the size of a tiger. The length is taken in a straight line between the end of the bony ridge which surmounts the braincase—to a point above the incisor teeth. On this basis the tigers of the Nepal Terai show a slight superiority in size over the tigers of Central and Southern India; though tigers as large as any North Indian animal may be found in Kanara or further south. The weight of a tiger averages between 400 and 500 lbs. Individuals far exceeding this weight have been shot. Females are smaller in build. The average length of a tigress is 8 ft. 6 in. The average weight about a 100 lbs. less than the male. Four to five hundred pounds of flesh and bone express the tiger's massive build. Yet, his heavy frame is cast in lines of perfect symmetry and endowed with astonishing suppleness of movement. His massive head, his muscular body, which even in repose reveals the immensity of its latent strength, his rich colouring give the tiger a magnificence which is unequalled by any of the great cats.

Kinship between the Lion and the Tiger.

There is a close kinship between the Lion and the Tiger. There is so much individual variation in both animals that it is difficult to find any constant point of difference in the skeletal structure of the two. What is written in description of one will apply equally to the other. On the average the skull of a tiger is more vaulted and has narrower nasal bones. The facial part of the skull is shorter in relation to the cranial portion. This gives the tiger a greater flatness of face when compared to the lion. The differences between the two are mainly skin deep. Even the tiger-like pattern of many lion cubs indicates the close kinship between the two animals. The mane, so associated with the lion, is not constant in that animal and many tigers wear a ruff of lengthy hairs about the neck and face which is as full as the mane of some lions.

The Tiger in India.

In India the tiger is found under varying conditions of climate and environment. He has left his tracks in the winter snows of the Himalayas at an altitude of 10,000 ft. He lives in humid evergreen forest or in dry open jungle, in grassy swamps or in an amphibious terrain of trees and mud and water.

No statistics are available to give an idea of the number of tigers living in different provinces in India. The opening of the country to settlement, the extermination of game animals, has driven the tiger from districts where he was once common. Where tigers are still found, their numbers probably fluctuate. Though supreme in his forests, the tiger is but one of a community of animals living within a particular area, and is so governed by all those forces which regulate the constantly varying density of its animal population. Changes in the environment in which the animal community lives, the inter-relationships existing between its members are some of the factors which control the number of animals living in a given locality. The hot weather with its scarcity of grazing and water supply may cause a concentration of cattle and game in a favoured locality and with it, a concentration of animals which prey upon them. The monsoon effecting a complete change in plant life, in water supply, in the abundance of parasites, results in a greater dispersal of animals. Factors such as these may reduce or increase the number of tigers living in a given area. Given continuity of favourable conditions a tiger may settle in a favoured locality for an indefinite period and establish his rights within his territory. On his death, his domain is taken over sooner or later by a successor.

Three things are essential to the tiger's territory—the neighbourhood of animals of a size commensurate with his needs, ample shade to sleep in, and water to quench his thirst. An emigrant from cooler northern climes, centuries of acclimatization have left him still intolerant to tropical heat. The tiger needs shelter under cave or covert in the day time from the heat, his pads may blister from long contact with the fiery ground, and many of his kind, particularly during the hot weather take to water and lie in it during the hot hours of the day. In common with many nocturnal animals, should the day be cold or clouded with rain, tigers may be up and about. Always their movements must be regulated by the animals upon which they prey. Like them the tiger is nocturnal. But should game be wanting or the opportunity to take cattle by night—hunger may compel a change of habit and make the tiger hunt by day.

How Tigers Hunt.

Ordinarily the tiger when hungry goes out to seek his food shortly before sunset and ends his hunting at break of day. He will go through cover if need be, but, like most forest animals he prefers the beaten track. He follows the accustomed trail of game, or takes a jungle path, road, a forest fire-line, or an open water course. In the gathering dusk he moves slowly and silently, stopping now and then. His acute hearing makes him conscious of any sound which betrays the presence of his quarry. His eyes attuned to work in the dark—detect the slightest movement, though like all cats, the tiger is less quick in the recognition of objects which are still. Many writers of experience maintain that a tiger hunts with his ears and eyes and makes little use of an enfeebled sense of smell. While the consensus of opinion appears to uphold this view—there are other factors which require consideration. There are those observers who have seen a tiger pick up the fresh ground scent of an animal, and turn in his course to follow it. Another tiger has followed the scent of a wounded quarry and yet another was observed to trace a kill which was dragged from its site. The behaviour of a particular tiger under given circumstances—his failure to discover his food by scent, to wind a man sitting in a tree—provides no evidence that tigers do not use their sense of smell. It is a faculty of no small importance to a beast of prey. To live a tiger has to find, to outwit and to overcome his prey. He must do all this in competition with his own kind and he is compelled to secure his quarry under varying circumstances wherein any one of his faculties may be at disadvantage and wherein success will imply a reliance on others. We know little as to the extent to which nocturnal animals rely on vision in getting their food. We know less about the inner working of the animal mind—we attempt to read it from external behaviour—behaviour which must vary with the individual and with circumstances. It is probable that all the tiger's senses play their purpose in his life—the predominance of any one of his faculties depends upon the individual and equally upon the factors in the environment which are then influencing his action.

In his quest for food the tiger's progress is described as the 'flowing past of a phantom'. His sinuous gliding movement is effected by the simultaneous advance of the limbs on each side of his body. Ordinarily his feet on each side leave a double track, the impression of the hind foot being a little in advance of the fore-foot. The imprint of the fore-foot is larger, rounder and more splayed out than that of the hind. The difference is usually less marked in the spoor of a tigress.

But the type of spoor a tiger leaves varies with the gait of the individual and depends equally upon what the tiger is doing. A slowing down of movement impelled by rousing interest on increased caution may sometimes be read in the reduction of space between the imprints of the fore- and hind-feet. The reduction may end in the feet imprinting a single track, the hind foot being placed over the exact spot vacated by the fore foot. But this is not the impress of care free movement but of highly controlled and deliberate action.

A tiger hunts by stealth. He stalks his animal or lying hidden takes it as it strays within reach. Whether cattle-killer or hunter of wild game, the tiger is accustomed to the habits of his prey and knows how and when and where to find it. His habit is to hunt alone. When in a family party his hunting may be in the nature of a drive; the tiger trying to rush the quarry in the direction of another lying concealed. Such combined hunts are frequent among lions. They have been less frequently observed among tigers.

The Killing of the Prey.

A tiger follows no rule in the killing of his prey. He passes from the awkward attempts of the young to the power and mastery of the adult. Equally must he adapt his strategy to the nature of his quarry and the conditions of its taking. There is the haphazard seizure of an animal in flight where desperate claws and teeth strive to retain and hold the moving body, or the timely leap, which takes the quarry in its stride and sends it to the ground—its neck broken by its fall and the opposing wrench of the tiger's hold. Different must be the killing of a standing animal. There are two common ways in which a tiger does this. Coming with slow deliberate approach or bewildering rush he dips under and takes his prey by the throat, draws down and pins its head to the ground and maintaining the pressure of his grasp, strangles his animal. Or, rearing up on his hind legs, he seizes the animal's neck in his jaws and bringing his arms down about its head and shoulders, takes it in violent hold and bears it to the ground. The ferocity of his strangle hold, his ruthless violence in forcing his prey to earth may twist the neck of a heavy animal, or bend it back upon itself till it breaks under the strain and the opposing stress from the body as it falls or is forced to the ground. The neck is not always broken. To break the neck of his prey is not perhaps a tiger's deliberate purpose. Like all the big cats he tries to take his animal by the neck or throat and strangle it. The neck, when broken, breaks from the manner of its seizure, the force exerted and most frequently from the opposing strain of the falling body.

A large animal may be seized by the hind leg. The leg is bitten into above the hock, its tendons severed and the bone broken. With one or both legs broken, bison, tsaine or buffalo despite their bulk and power, fall easy victims. They are killed as they weaken. Tigers in Burma invariably break the legs of a large animal before killing it. The method is less common in India. It is suggested that the more open nature of forests in India gives the clearance a tiger needs for his normal point of attack—the neck or throat. Not much blood is shed in the tiger's process of killing. His jaws maintain their grip, though his animal is dead and its struggles have ceased. The fangs buried in the flesh obstruct the flow and prevent the spilling of much blood. There is no evidence to show that the tiger sucks the blood of his prey.

The Tiger and his Kill.

A tiger brings to his eating the same ferocity and lust which he displays in the killing of his quarry. Savagery when feeding, a common trait in animals, is a demonstration against possible interference. With it, the tiger combines a wild animal's instinctive anticipation of danger. When feeding, or coming to his kill, any sound the reason for which is not apparent may cause the tiger to disappear like a flash. While he desires to hold what he has, his instinct for self-preservation predominates, as it predominates in all animals. Cowardice or bravery, both human characteristics are inappropriate to the description of animal behaviour. Animals do not possess an exalted ethical code. Strong or weak, they normally obey the primary instinct which is to preserve life. Endangering life in defence of themselves is but obedience to the same instinct. Though supreme in his jungles, the one rival a tiger must fear is another tiger who can take his food from him and destroy him in the taking. He fears and avoids Man, but competition from his own kind is the more intimate factor in his struggle for existence. This explains the common impulse of the tiger to drag his kill under cover where he can eat it in greater seclusion—though freedom from interference may induce or circumstances compel him to feed in the open. In eating, his first and most usual choice is the hind quarters. In this he differs from the Leopard whose custom is to start his meal in the region of the breast bone or stomach. Like the lion, a tiger generally disembowels the body and places the entrails to one side. It may take a tiger the best part of two hours to finish the hind quarters of a bullock and a hungry tiger may eat the greater part of the body at a single meal. The remains of the carcase are left exposed or dragged and hidden under bushes or even concealed with uprooted bunches of grass when no cover is near. The tiger's neglect or care of his preserve of food must depend much upon the density or openness of the country in which he is accustomed to hunt, and the chances or frequency of interference with his kills by vultures and animals which discover and eat it. The abundance or scarcity of food may equally govern his actions.

After satisfying his hunger the tiger goes to drink and then to sleep either in the vicinity of his kill or away from it. Freedom from disturbance, conditions of cover, the need for cool shelter are all factors which influence his behaviour. When darkness sets in or even earlier he returns to his kill and may continue to repeat his visits till the carcase is finished. Or, for various reasons he abandons his quarry.

From hunger or individual preference a tiger may eat a carcase not of his killing however putrid. His usual habit is to feed on his prey when killed. He may even feed on a crippled animal before life is extinct. Ordinarily a period, which may be anything between 4 and 7 days, elapses between successive kills. There is sometimes a simultaneous killing of a number of individuals in a herd of cattle. It is generally the work of a young tiger or of a female with cubs.

Cattle, various species of deer, nilghai, pig and porcupine are the common prey of the tiger. Larger animals like bison, tsaine and wild buffalo, bear and leopard are killed occasionally. Tigers living near villages are said to feed largely on cattle. Whether cattle killing becomes habitual in the individual is not definitely known. It may develop in an individual with age, when the taking of more active and vigilant prey becomes difficult. Unlike the panther, the tiger's association with Man is limited to forest areas, where a variety of food is available and wherein limitation to domestic prey becomes less imperative. It is significant that certain districts in Southern India, where cattle are in abundance, but where deer and other large game are now all but exterminated, are now devoid of tigers, which suggest that the presence or absence of game is a factor in the tiger's selection of a habitat.

The tiger is not usually dangerous to man except when wounded or perhaps under stress of sexual excitement. A tigress with cubs may make a demonstration of frightfulness, charge home or even desert her cubs.

The man-eating tiger is fortunately uncommon. Insufficiency of natural food or causes which prevent the securing of it may convert a tiger into a man-eater. The vice is acquired in age or in youth. The chance killing of a man may initiate the habit in a young animal, or an old or disabled tiger may take to man hunting. Familiarity with the presence of Man subdues his fear, and hunger compels him to attack what his experiment discovers to be the easiest prey. Man-eating appears to be more frequent in females. Difficulty in finding sufficient food for the cubs suggests a reason. Such cubs trained to the vice by their parents may retain the habit through life. In individual instances man hunting like cattle killing, may be a tradition passed on from mother to offspring. This perhaps is the explanation of the repeated occurrence of man-eaters in certain districts of India and their comparative rarity in others where tigers are equally or perhaps more common.

The Calls of Tigers.

In many of his habits the tiger resembles the Lion, but a tiger is more silent. Tigers seldom roar. When they do, their roars can be deceptively like the roar of a lion. Deep and thrilling, the repeated gusts of sound increase in volume and fill the air with their reverberations. This roaring is said to be a mate call. It is sometimes uttered when the tiger rouses at dusk preparatory to going out or while in quest for food. There is the coughing roar which may prelude attack and the 'whoof' which expresses surprise and alarm and a purring note made by blowing air through the lips with which he gives vent to when expressing contentment.

A peculiar call of the tiger, which is much like the belling of a sambhar, has occasioned much comment. The calls of the two animals are so similar that it is difficult to distinguish between them in forests where both tiger and sambhar live. This peculiar call is not the tiger's ruse to decoy a sambhar. It has no concern with his hunting. One suggested explanation is that it is a mate call. The tiger utters it when seeking or keeping in touch with a mate. It is indicated however that the call has been frequently uttered as a direct result of disturbance by human agency and as such is purely an individual expression of surprise, suspicion or alarm.

The Mating and Breeding of Tigers.

The tiger is by nature a solitary and unsociable animal. The bond which brings and keeps tigers together is the reproductive instinct and the subsequent care of the young. This is the general basis of social life in all the lower animals. In India many tigers seem to mate after the rains and the majority of young are born between February and May. We do not know whether the tiger is monogamous. The acquiring of more than one mate will depend, among other factors, on the number of females in condition to breed and the dominance of a particular tiger over other males in the area. Tigers with more than one adult female in train have been seen. Whether the association between a male and female is ever permanent is not known. It appears to end or to be interrupted when the cubs are born. The summary treatment of the cubs by the male may induce the mother's desire for seclusion at this period. It has been observed however that a family party consisting of a tigress and her cubs frequently includes an adult male. The presence of the male may suggest an uninterrupted association of the parents or it may indicate the renewal of sexual activity in the female and the acquiring of a mate. We have no definite knowledge regarding the cycles of sexual periodicity in the larger Felidae. It is suggested that tigers breed after intervals of not less than two or three years, the period during which the cubs live under parental protection. The mother may however be accompanied by cubs of more than one litter—the previous cubs are then fairly well grown and almost in a condition to fend for themselves.

The period of gestation is fifteen weeks. The tigress gives birth to cubs in the jungle, or in a cave or rough shelter of rocks. As many as six cubs may be born in a litter—usually not more than 2 or 3 survive. The cubs are soon able to wander about their lair and when about six months old regularly accompany the mother. The largest family party seen by Mr. Dunbar Brander consisted of an adult male, two full grown females and three cubs nearly as large as the tigress. Such a family party in quest for food may hunt in co-operation—the hunt assuming the nature of the drive. The practice is more common with family parties of lions and provides an opportunity for the training of the young. That the mother tigress trains her cubs to hunt has been observed. Her method is to disable an animal so that it cannot escape the onslaught of her cubs who come in and take a share in the killing. It is probably at this period that the tendencies of the individual to cattle or game killing or even man hunting are formed.

Various observations on the behaviour of individuals have given us our impression of the tiger and the rôle it plays in Nature. With the facts that we gather we attempt to predict what an animal *will do*. This is the aim of our observation. While the individual animal obeys the fixed instincts of its species, its behaviour is influenced by parental tradition—by the experience it acquires through life, by its physical environment, by its changing relationships with the animal community in which it lives. Our knowledge of the true life of the tiger can only come to us by a greater knowledge of the factors which influence its life. We must study not only the animal but also the stage upon which it plays its rôle. We have still to learn more about the tiger's reactions to the varied conditions of its physical environment, to climate, to season, to new situations and to the animal community in which it lives. We have still to learn about its migrations and movements, its sexual relations and its social life. Such knowledge can only come as the result of continued field observation, and more especially from controlled systematic investigation—surely worthwhile in an animal which plays so definite a rôle in the economy of Nature in this country, and which is so surrounded with immemorial romance and interest.

THE PANTHER (*PANTHERA PARDUS* LINN.).

Panther is a word of Greek and Latin derivation meaning 'all animals'. Greek and Roman writers applied it to many predatory creatures, among others the Cheetah, the Weasel and the Lynx. From common usage it is now a recognised name for the Leopard in India.

In its structure a panther exemplifies all those characters which unite and distinguish the Great Cats (*Pantherina*) from the rest of their tribe. It has been shown that in Lions, Tigers, Panthers, Jaguars and in the Ounce, the hyoid bone is loosely attached to the skull as a result of the imperfect ossification of the arms of this apparatus. In all these animals the pupil of the eye does not narrow to a slit, but retains its circular form when contracting. Again in all of them the patch of horn-sheathed spines on the surface of the tongue displays a distinctive position. Now if the skulls of a lion, tiger, panther or jaguar are compared it will be found that they are very similar in form. Except for differences in size and a few slight specific characters there is little to distinguish between the skulls of these animals. Agreement in their skeletal structure suggests their close affinity.

It is true that the Panther and the Jaguar have disinctive colour patterns. But young lions are also spotted or striped and the vestiges of the panther's 'rosettes' are sometimes developed in the markings of a tiger. Colour differences between these animals are less fundamental than they appear.

Panthers and jaguars are lower in stature than tigers or lions. They are less massive in build, longer in body and more lithe in limb. These distinctions are probably associated with their tree-climbing habits. Their roars are remarkably alike but normally quite different from the roaring of lions and tigers. It is believed that the Panther and the Jaguar are descended from a common ancestral stock which originated in Europe or North Asia: that the progenitors of the Jaguar probably migrated into America by way of Northern Asia and established the species in the New World.

Distribution of the Panther.

The primeval forests of Europe and North Asia are indicated as the region from which the Lion, the Tiger, the Panther and the Jaguar spread into various countries which they now inhabit.

Fossil remains of panthers, indistinguishable from those now living have been found in the cave deposits of the Pleistocene Age in Spain, France, Germany and England. At the present time the Panther survives in Europe only in the Russian Province of Kuban, north of the Caucasus. But its territory covers practically the whole of Africa and Asia.

In Asia its range extends from Palestine and Syria through Persia to Manchuria and Korea. Southward its territory reaches through China into Burma, the Malay Peninsula and Java and covers practically the whole of India and Ceylon.

Whether the Panther established itself in India before the

Lion, we do not know. It may have accompanied or preceded it. Both animals probably entered India from the West. But like the Tiger, the Panther may have also migrated into India through the hill ranges of Assam. That it established itself in Peninsular India before the Tiger is suggested by its occupation of the Island of Ceylon, where tigers are not found. Earlier colonisation of the Peninsula may have enabled the Panther to enter Ceylon over the land-bridge which once connected the Island with the main land. The Tiger's passage, it is presumed, was prevented by the disappearance of this bridge.

Variations in Panthers.

Through the extent of a range covering two Continents there is but one species of panther, living under contrasting conditions of environment, of climate, temperature and rainfall. Such varied conditions of life may have influenced the minor but more or less apparent distinctions seen among panthers in different countries. Variation is especially marked in Asiatic panthers whose colour may range from the sandy grey of the Persian panther to the golden yellow of the Indian and the rusty red of the Javanese animal. Distinctions are also seen in the boldness, the spacing and the size of the rosettes and in the texture, length and density of the coat.

Eleven more or less distinct races or varieties of panther are recognised in Asia. Three are found within the Indian Empire.

The Kashmir Panther (*Panthera pardus millardi*) is distinguished from the Indian by its softer, more furry coat, its grey buff colouring, its small, close-set, thick rimmed rosettes.

The Sind Panther (*Panthera pardus sindica*) is known only from the barren Khirthar hills of the Sind-Baluch border. Its coat is thick, but harsh and rough; its colouring brighter than the sandy grey of a Persian panther but distinctly more pale than the average Indian animal.

The Indian Panther (*Panthera pardus fusca*) ranges from the Himalayas to Cape Comorin and Ceylon. As far as is known, it is indistinguishable from panthers found in Assam and Burma. A typical panther from the Indian Peninsula is a sleek short haired animal with a fulvous or bright fulvous coat, marked with small, close-set rosettes. There is however considerable variation of colour in Indian panthers. At present it is not possible to define the limits of such variation or to correlate it with particular areas. Panthers living in dense evergreen forests are generally richer in colouring than those found in drier open country. In the forests of Burma the ground colour of the Panther is generally a bright chestnut.

Among abnormal phases of colour, black is the commonest. The black of a panther's coat may be as deep as the black of its spots, which are then only discernible in bright light. The black may extend to the tongue and in varying degrees to the gums and palate. The eyes are sometimes a curious blue. A black panther is not a distinct species. Black and normal coloured cubs may be produced by the same parent. The abnormal colour is due to the excessive presence of a pigment called melanin which darkens the hair and other parts of the body. Melanism is common among animals which have a supra abundance of this pigment. The condition is common in panthers, exceptional in tigers. Tigers on the other hand reveal a greater tendency to albinism a condition opposite to melanism in which the dark pigment is entirely or partly wanting. Albino tigers are not uncommon; albino panthers very rare. Melanism like albinism may arise as an individual variation, but when either condition appears in many individuals in a given area, it is probably due to germinal variation, and inter-breeding among such individuals results in the perpetuation of melano or albino forms; particularly if preferential mating takes place. This is instanced perhaps in the successive generations of white tigers in the Rewa State and the comparative abundance of black panthers in certain areas. The causes which give rise to melanism are not known. Black panthers are rarely found in drier and more open country. One is recorded from the Central Provinces and one from Idar State. They are plentiful in Java and in the Southern parts of the Malay Peninsula, and are known from the evergreen forests of Burma, Assam, Nepal and South-Western India. They are quite common in the forests of Malabar. Whether the colour of a black panther is adaptive to the darker conditions of these dense forests, we do not know. Its coat is without obvious pattern. The spotted coat of a panther blends with the checkered light and shade of the jungle by day and converts it into an evanescent phantom in the darkness or in moonlight. Yet both black and spotted panthers thrive in the same forests, suggesting that pattern may be of no essential significance in life of the animal.

There is marked variation in size among Indian Panthers. Some grow to the size of small tigers, others are scarcely larger than some of the lesser cats, though fully adult. It is suggested that differences in size may have some relation to the habits of the animal and that in the Central Provinces and in the drier parts of the Peninsula panthers which live habitually on game within the forests are larger than those which seek their food about towns and villages. Dunbar Brander gives the average dimensions of a forest panther as 7 ft. 5 in. and its weight at about 150 lbs.

On the other hand small panthers are generally common in the hill forests of South India and in the more wooded portions of the Himalayas. The panthers which frequent the cliffs and precipices of the Anamallais and Nelliampathies are distinctively small in build and size. The smallest race is said to be found in the forests of Java.

The average size of a male Indian Panther is 6 ft. 8 in. The tail varies much in length; its length when included with body measurements may give a wrong impression of the size of an otherwise poorly-built animal. Separate measurements of head and body, and of the tail should always be recorded.

Distinctions in size and in the shape of the skull have led to the belief that there are two species of panther in India. Such differences are due mainly to sex. The skull of the adult male panther is larger with larger teeth. Its cranial portion is more elongate, less rounded than in the female and carries a more prominent median crest.

While there is local variation among panthers there is also individual variation affecting both structure and colouring. Individuals sometime exhibit a complete disintegration of markings far exceeding similar deviations in pattern in tigers. So complete may be the fusing and breaking up of the spots, that a particular skin obtained in South Kanara gives the impression of a black panther streaked and spotted with yellow.

The Panther and its Environment.

The Panther, as we have seen, is found over an immense range of territory, covering practically the whole of Asia and Africa. In practice an animal is limited in its distribution, by its habits and its reactions. Its reactions to environment and other influences are so adjusted that it chooses places to live in which are suitable to its needs. A tiger's range is limited by its need for the shade and shelter of forest, for continuous tracts of cover. The lion chooses drier, more open country. Both tigers and lions require the propinquity of large animals for food. A panther is less bound by the physical condition of its environment. It is more tolerant of the sun than the tiger and less dependent on shelter from its heat or on the nearness of a water supply. It thrives in a parched treeless terrain of rock and scrub or in rain swept forests, under extremes of heat and cold, of dryness or humidity.

A panther can subsist on a variety of small creatures which would give no adequate sustenance to a tiger. It can find shelter and security in the scantiest cover. Its adaptiveness to varied conditions of life enable it to overcome those factors which limit the increase and confine the range of lions and tigers.

Diversity in conditions of life produce in the panthers a variation in food and habits.

The Village Panther.

Very considerable must be the influence of Man on the life and habits of the species. The panther's ability to live under conditions where no tiger would survive brings it into freer and more constant touch with Man. As such it is able to profit to a greater extent from such opportunities of food getting as are provided by human agency. As such it has become a greater potential scourge on human life and human property. The panther living near human settlements, particularly outside forest areas preys mainly on domestic animals—on cattle, sheep and goats, on ponies and donkeys and most commonly on dogs. It finds regular opportunity to take grazing cattle, to intercept stragglers from flocks and herds returning home at dusk, to raid cattle pens and enclosures or carry off dogs at night. For the village panther the problem of food getting is simplified. The food is concentrated within a limited area, the occasions for taking it are more or less constant and identical. Further competition for the food is frequently reduced by the elimination of rival beasts of prey for whom the environment is unsuitable, and the prey itself, its alertness enfeebled by domestication, is easily secured. The influence of these conditions on the life of the Panther vary in their effects on the individual. Domestic prey if easily taken must be taken in conflict with Man and such competition usually develops great boldness, cunning and resource in animals. We have come to associate these attributes with the Panther because of their frequent and singular development in panthers living under the educative influence of human association. Nevertheless association with Man seldom changes a panther's instinctive habit of concealment. Secrecy and stealth are the essence of its hunting. Whether it lives in remote forests or in the neighbourhood of towns and villages it maintains its secretive nature, is rarely seen and hunts mainly under cover of darkness.

Faced with the sudden apparition of man in regions rarely entered by him, a panther or a tiger usually reveal no more than the wild beasts' curiosity or suspicion of the unknown. Ordinarily they betray no undue fear, stare a while at the intruder and go quietly away. Experience gained from association with Man may exaggerate this reaction in a panther, may develop in it great fear and suspicion. While familiarity with Man, success in escaping harm, will beget in another outrageous boldness, an indifference to human activity, to lights, sounds or movements, and a disregard for human presence even in broad daylight.

Panthers living near human settlements probably maintain this mode of life through successive generations. For the life of the animal is not only the sum of its fixed instincts—a legacy born of the experience of countless ancestors—but also of parental tradition and of experience acquired in life. Hence many village panthers have come to rely mainly on human agency for their food supply. When the supply is maintained it may lead individuals to establish more or less permanent territory in the neighbourhood of towns and villages, and an interruption or failure in the supply to migration to similar environment where the accustomed food is available. While the type of prey the panther is accustomed to hunt is largely a matter of individual habit and upbringing, these habits are induced in parent and offspring by the conditions of their habitat. Changes in the nature of the habitat must produce a transition in habits of life leading from a more or less complete dependence on domestic animals for food to increasing or complete reliance on wild animals as prey.

The Game-killing Panther.

Conditions of life for panthers which live entirely by the killing of wild creatures must be different. Their prey is more varied in character and habit. It is not concentrated within limited zones. It is less sedentary. Seasonal and other changes in the environment influence its concentration or dispersal in a given area. Such changes in the density of the animal population living within a given area bring about the wider ranging habits of beasts of prey.

Equally, as in the case of village panthers, a continuity of favourable conditions must lead an individual or a pair to establish hunting rights over a territory sufficiently large to supply food requirements.

Apart from these influences there is the factor of increased competition. Forest areas which support a large and varied assemblage of herbivorous animals equally make possible the co-existence of a varied assemblage of predatory species. Now competition between various carnivores is governed by the size of the prey to which each is more or less limited. The herbivorous species form what is called a 'food chain'. Commencing with the smallest forms predators and prey increase in size so that at the end of the chain we have the largest herbivorous animals which are the prey of the largest carnivores. The competition for food between the tiger and panther is thus governed to some extent by the size of the prey to which each is more or less limited. While the tiger and panther are at the same end of the 'food chain' the panther occupies a lower link. The panther must equally face the competition of its own species and in certain areas it is brought into competition with some of the larger cats, like the Clouded Leopard, and the Golden Cat which take a similar prey.

Again, while the strength and prowess of the predator decides the size and nature of its prey, there are some species like wolves and wild dogs which increase their effective size by the strategy of numbers and are able to enter into competition with panthers or tigers.

These are some of the factors which must influence the life and food getting habits of panthers particularly of those individuals whose conditions of life remain unaltered by the artificial influence of human association. The collection of more concise data concerning the panther's reaction to varying environment, to the animal community in which it lives, to competition with Man and other rivals, its migrations, movements, its acquirement of territory would help us to truer understanding of the life and habits of the animal.

The Panther's Method of Hunting.

Mr. Dunbar Brander indicates that panthers in the forests of the Central Provinces which confine themselves to the killing of wild animals display many of the habits and ways of a tiger. In other words they display the truer habits of their species. Their prey consists of various kinds of deer and antelopes, of monkeys, pigs and porcupines. When food is scarce even birds or reptiles are eaten. Like the tiger, the forest panther follows roads or paths or the beaten track of animals through the forest, or waits in hiding for its prey. It seizes its quarry from the ground or leaps upon it from a height such as an overhanging branch. Deer and other animals following their accustomed path are sometimes taken in this way. Monkeys are hunted in the tree tops.

Watching the movements of its quarry from some elevated perch or rise is a common method of hunting. Wild sheep and goats feeding on open hill sides or village cattle in the plain are frequently watched and stalked from such a position. The panther has a keen eyesight and an acute sense of hearing. Its sense of smell is said to be better developed than a tiger's. Opinions differ on this point.

To take its prey by surprise is the basis of the panther's strategy. Its purpose is effected by noiseless approach, an amazing capacity for concealment and a lightning agility in attack. Failure to surprise its quarry and to seize it in the first attempt frequently results in the panther's discomfiture and retreat, even before so humble a quarry as a goat. Tigers reveal a similar trait in their hunting and usually relinquish their prey if they do not succeed in taking it in the initial attack. This is a common trait in the hunting of Cats. A panther's quarry if not small enough to be pounced upon and carried off is seized by the throat and held in a strangle hold. To kill their prey by strangling it is apparently the purpose of the great Cats. The breaking of the victim's neck may or may not follow as result of the seizure. A large and exceptionally powerful panther may break the neck of an animal in the violence and fury of its onslaught. Usually death is caused by strangulation, and may ensue without the infliction of fatal wounds.

As with the tiger, there is no evidence to show that a panther sucks the blood of its prey. Like the tiger it maintains its grip for some time to ensure death. A premature release, as happens when a panther is shot while holding down its prey has resulted in the recovery of the victim.

The Panther and its Kill.

The panther's usual impulse after killing is to drag the carcase under cover to eat it where there is no danger of disturbance. In obedience to this impulse individuals have displayed remarkable ingenuity, eating through the neck or leg of a tethered animal to carry it away. A panther usually commences his meal at the stomach or in the region of the breast bone. The viscera, the flesh of the ribs and the fore quarters are first eaten. The neck and head are left to the last. The unconsumed portion of a panther's kill, if seen early, is remarkably even and clear in outline. The ribs appear as though trimmed with a butcher's knife. A panther may commence his meal on a large animal between the buttocks in the accustomed manner of a tiger. This is said to be the practice of large game-killing panthers. As with the tiger, the unconsumed portion of the carcase is usually dragged and concealed under bushes, put away among the boulders of a nullah or a deliberate attempt is made to cover it with leaves and grass. Though plenty of ground cover is available some individuals prefer to carry and place the kill in a tree. Particular trees may become the regular resorts to which the resident panther of the neighbourhood takes his reserve of food for safe storage. The feat of scrambling up a tree with a full grown cheetal stag in its mouth gives an idea of the strength and resource of an individual panther. Man-eating panthers who have developed this habit may dispose of their kills in the same way.

Dragging the kill away to eat it in hiding, concealing the

remains on the ground or in a tree are devices for the protection of the food from rivals. All beasts of prey will feed on any carcase they happen to discover. Besides professional hunters there are professional scavengers like hyaenas and jackals, vultures, crows and even eagles with plebean tastes. Food is the burning question in animal society and the habits of all animals are mainly directed to obtaining a sufficiency of it. Having provided for the security of its reserve of food, the panther usually lies up in its vicinity and returns to its kill when darkness approaches. It may return to its kill at any hour of the day, or it may abandon it altogether. Everything depends on the situation of the kill, if secluded or otherwise upon circumstances, upon the idiosyncrasies, the past experiences of the individual and the state of its appetite.

While some individuals display an almost reckless confidence in approach, a panther returning to its kill is usually the personification of cautiousness. The advance to the kill is slow and the panther's movements in its immediate neighbourhood highly controlled and deliberate. It surveys the surroundings both around the kill and in the trees above it. Anything unusual or abnormal may awaken its suspicion and cause an immediate retreat or abandonment of the meal. Boldness in returning to the kill after being shot at or otherwise disturbed is a matter of past experience, or temperament or hunger. A panther fired at over a kill does not necessarily connect the sound with any particular danger. The sudden report is alarming and puts the beast to flight but if no harm has come to him he usually returns.

The kill, as we have seen, is a source of attraction to a number of rivals dangerous or otherwise and the panther's natural instinct is to apprehend the possibility of interference. The existence of tigers in the same forest is a source of danger of which the panther is acutely conscious. Panthers have been destroyed at their kills by tigers or by more powerful rivals of their own species. They have been killed, routed or otherwise deprived of their rights to a meal by wild dogs and hyaenas. That a hyaena or wild dogs in company may be more than a match for a panther is shown by the number of recorded instances in which victory has gone to these animals. At the same time we read of wild dogs or a hyaena being driven from a kill by the onslaught of a panther. The circumstances of the encounter, the advantage of surprise and other factors, which may or may not be apparent to the observer give victory to one or the other of the contestants and obscure conclusions as to their respective prowess.

Very curious on the other hand is the behaviour of animals—habitual victims of the panther in the presence of their enemy at a kill. We read of cattle and deer continuing to graze unconcerned in close proximity to a panther absorbed in its meal. Their behaviour suggests that these animals appear to divine the presence or absence of hostile intent in a traditional enemy and react accordingly. It has been observed in Africa that zebra and other animals commonly hunted by lions are unaffected by their roars by day and seem to know exactly when these roars threaten danger and when they do not.

The Man-eating Panther.

Speaking generally, like the tiger, the panther does not attack man if unprovoked. If taken unawares a panther may attack in self-defence or turn on his pursuers as when wounded, or harried in a beat. The attack may be made in error, the panther mistaking man for more legitimate prey. This sometimes happens when people are moving or sitting in heavy cover. This chance killing of a man is suggested as one of the causes which lead panthers or tigers to man-eating. The diffidence to attack human beings once overcome may induce an individual to include human beings amongst its prey or may convert it into a habitual man-eater. While the confirmed man-eating panther is fortunately rare the number which occasionally take human food is not inconsiderable.

Failure in the accustomed food supply or in the ability to obtain it contributes to the making of a man-eater. One of the after results of the great famine in Gujerat between 1901-1903 was a marked increase in the number of man-eating tigers and panthers.

The village panther unable to obtain its usual food may take to man-killing. In the recorded case of one individual whose accustomed prey was dogs and cattle, the first victim was a baby, the second an old woman, and the third a boy. Emboldened with its success, such a panther first limiting itself to taking people asleep outside their huts, takes to entering huts, to carrying off people sitting up by a fire and finally to killing in broad daylight. Brought into more intimate touch with Man, the man-eating panther is not only more frequent than the man-eating tiger but more to be dreaded. Familiarity with Man and his ways makes it bolder, more difficult to circumvent and gives it greater capacity for destruction.

The Call of the Panther.

The commonest call of the panther is a succession of deep intakes of air and hoarse barking coughs—an interval of a second separating each respiratory effort. The call is made with the mouth partly open. The air inhaled and expelled through the trumpet-like cavity of the throat beats against the transverse ridges of the palate which, it is suggested, possibly play a part in increasing the sonority of the tone. The call is usually likened to sound produced by the thrust and return of a coarse-toothed saw cutting through thin wood. A pair of panther cubs in captivity gave vent to this distinctive sawing call when moved by the prospect of a meal or when separated from one another. The occasions when they used it may suggest a similar usage in the adults. Among other sounds made by panthers is the low deep threatening growl which is the preliminary intimation of a charge by a wounded or angry beast. The two or three deep coughs which may accompany the charge are very similar to the sounds made by a tiger in like circumstances. A soft purring 'gr-gr', at times hardly perceptible is occasionally emitted in the vicinity of a 'kill' and there is, as in the case of the tiger, the 'whoof' with which a panther expresses alarm and disapproval when surprised and rushing off.

The Mating and Breeding of Panthers.

Panthers like tigers breed all the year round. Mating has been observed in various months of the year. It is a common belief that most animals have well demarcated breeding seasons. Critical investigation has shown that a relatively large number breed throughout the year. This is particularly true in the case of tropical animals. When a species has a demarcated breeding season it recurs rhythmically at the same time every year. The quiescent reproductive organs of the male become active while the female undergoes cycles of reproductive activity. As a general rule, the sexual periodicity of the male is the counterpart of the female's: but with some species the male season may begin earlier than the female or the male may remain reproductively potent throughout the year, while the female experiences cycles of sexual activity and quiescence. The reverse may also occur. We have no definite knowledge as regards sexual periodicity in the larger Felidae. We do not know whether the males are sexually potent throughout the year nor do we know anything about the cycles of sexual activity in the females. In a lioness in captivity periods of heat about a week in duration occurred at intervals of three weeks till the animal became pregnant. Whether similar condition obtain among the larger felines in the wild state remains to be discovered. Such information is extremely difficult to obtain particularly in relation to animals in the wild state. When animals are shot, microscopic examination in the field of the fresh contents of the reproductive organs in both may shed some light on the points raised. It cannot be doubted that a mass of interesting details remains to be discovered which would give us a clearer understanding of the breeding habits and social life of these animals.

The intervals at which panthers produce a litter in the wild state are not definitely known. A pair of panthers in captivity had three litters in 3½ years. That sexual activity in the female recurs shortly after the production of a litter is instanced in the case of a female accompanied by two cubs computed to be above two, but not more than 6 months old. The parent which was shot during the month of May was found to contain four foetuses. If the age of the cubs was correctly estimated and if we set their age at the estimated maximum of 6 months, then her cubs were born approximately in December. The period of gestation being 3 months, a second litter would have been produced approximately at the end of July. This gives an interval of nine months between the production of two litters. The case may or may not be exceptional but it points to a potentially high rate of breeding among panthers which is probably one of the reasons why the species maintains its numbers in spite of all the efforts to reduce them.

Having acquired a mate there is little reticence in the courting of the panther. The procreative instinct overcomes all accustomed considerations for silence and secrecy. Their mating is accompanied by noisy demonstrations, by snarling and spasmodic roarings and by intervals of play, of gamboling and chasing dictated by the receptive or resentive attitude of the female. Mating may continue even after pregnancy is well established. There is a record of a pair seen cohabiting, the female when shot, was found to be bearing three foetuses about two weeks old. It is believed that the association of the male and female continues when the cubs are born. Whether it is ever permanent is not known. In the tiger it is believed that the association is interrupted at this stage. We have seen that among panthers sexual activity may recur shortly after a litter is produced. In these circumstances the male may be the original partner or a new-found mate. Mr. R. C. Morris has seen a family of 6 panthers consisting of an adult male and female, 2 three-quarter grown cubs and 2 cubs (about 2 months old). The adult male was possibly not the father of the larger cubs. That a female losing her mate will in favourable circumstances promptly take another is seen in the case of a panther acquiring a fresh partner twenty-four hours after the death of her previous mate.

The period of gestation is said to be about 12 weeks. Two to four cubs are usually produced. The mother chooses a cave, the hollow trunk of a tree, an overhanging rock or even a porcupine's earth as a shelter for her litter. She is assiduous in her care of them and is said to display greater determination in their defence than is usually seen in the tiger. Nothing precise is known about the period of lactation or when the cubs are weaned or how long they continue to live with their parents or when they attain maturity. Females accompanied by cubs almost as large as the parent have been frequently observed. From an early age the cubs display their predatory instincts, going through the process of crouching, stalking and springing at one another in the manner of the adult. As with the lions and tigers the mother is said to watch the early attempts of the young in making a kill. Col. Mosse records his observation of the behaviour of a female with a cub about as large as herself at a kill. The cub was all concentration while the mother affected complete indifference to the tethered bait and changed her position only to get a better view of the efforts of the cub. The conflict between the impatience of youth and the instinct for cautious approach was strikingly apparent in the efforts of the cub to stalk its quarry. The interesting *denouement* was unfortunately prevented by a shot from the observer.

The high rate of breeding among panthers has already been indicated. Apart from this, the panther's wide range of food and its powers of resistance to adverse influences of environment have endowed it with those attributes which make for survival and which enable it to maintain its being over the vast range of territory which it inhabits. Man's efforts at extermination have made but little impression on its numbers in this country. Though it has not the magnificence of the tiger nor the imposing presence of the lion, the panther typifies in itself all the distinctive attributes of the Great Cats. It exhibits in perfection that symmetry of form, that combination of grace, strength and agility which distinguish its tribe. The panther is the embodiment of the ideal of a beast of prey.

THE SNOW LEOPARD OR OUNCE (*UNCIA UNCIA* SCHREBER).

The Snow Leopard is perhaps the most beautiful of all the cats. The soft colouring and luxuriant beauty of its fur, particularly in winter, is unrivalled. In common with all creatures to whom Nature has given a special endowment of beauty it pays the price in being persistently sought after and killed by Man.

The known range of the Snow Leopard is the high tablelands of Central Asia reaching northwards into the Altai Mountains and southwards to the Hindu Kush Mountains and the Great Himalayan Range.

An affinity between the Snow Leopard, the Lion, Tiger, Panther and Jaguar is deduced from a similarity in the structure of the hyoid apparatus in these animals. The Snow Leopard is placed in a separate genus because of peculiarities in the structure of its skull. Among the more obvious differences are the shortness of its muzzle, the elevation of the forehead and the vertical chin. A more fundamental distinction is seen in the structure of the auditory bullae—the bony swellings on the under surface of the skull, close to the ear openings. The auditory bulla of an Ounce is divided internally by a vertical partition into two nearly equal chambers. In the tiger, lion, panther and jaguar the chambers are unequal.

The ground colour of the Snow Leopard's coat is soft grey, paling to pure white on the underside. The spots are unbroken and distinct on the head, nape and lower parts of the limbs. On the body they break up into larger, paler rosettes. The rosettes are less distinctive in the more luxuriant fur of the winter coat; a black streak extends from the middle of the back to the root of the tail. Except for a few dark blotches the fur of the belly is pure white.

Little is known about the habits of the Snow Leopard. It is entirely nocturnal. During summer the animal lives in the higher altitudes of its range. It has been seen at a height of 18,000 ft. upwards. In this treeless region it preys on burhel, ibex and on marmots and other rodents, occasionally taking a calf or a sheep from the flocks grazing in the higher reaches during Summer. In Winter, Snow Leopards come down to the warmer valleys as low as 6,000 to 7,000 ft. where they find more frequent occasion to take domestic prey and offer better opportunity to be trapped or shot. Nothing is known about their breeding habits.

SUB-FAMILY II: *ACINONYCHINAE*.

THE CHEETAH OR HUNTING-LEOPARD (*ACINONYX JUBATUS* ERXLEBEN).

In India the Cheetah is all but extinct in the wild state. It once ranged from the confines of Bengal through the plains of the United Provinces, the Punjab and Rajputana, through Central India and the Deccan. It is not known to have occurred in South India and Ceylon. Evidence of its existence in recent years in some parts of its known range is seen in such records as the Society has been able to collect. A Cheetah was killed in 1918 and another in 1919 in the Mirzapur District of the United Provinces. Five Cheetahs are recorded as having been obtained in this Province during the previous twenty-five years. In the Central Provinces, the Cheetah appears to have been not uncommon at one time in the Berars. Three were shot in the Melghat Forest area in 1890 and one in 1894 and one at Wano in 1895. Rumours of their existence in parts of Berar, the Seoni Plateau and Saugor still persist. They were apparently once common around Hyderabad, Deccan. The only part of the Bombay Presidency where Cheetahs were known to occur recently is the tract of rugged country known as the Tanga in the centre of the province of Kathiawar. In 1884 it was estimated that there were not more than twenty of these animals in this area. A female and four cubs were shot at Rajkot in 1894.

Outside India, the range of the Cheetah is said to extend northwards to Russian Turkestan and Trans-Caspia. In South-Western Asia its range is believed to reach from the frontiers of Sind through parts of Afghanistan, Baluchistan and Persia and Mesopotamia to Syria and Palestine and thence into Africa, where cheetahs are, or were once found as far south as the Cape. To what extent it survives in these Asiatic countries is not known. There is a record of a female and cubs taken at Nasriyah in Mesopotamia in 1928, but the animal was not known to the local Arabs.

Certain peculiarities in the structure of a Cheetah differentiate it from all other cats. In size and form a Cheetah looks like a long-legged slender-bodied leopard. But its slimness of body and length of limb are equalled by some cats such as the African Serval. Its head is rounded and relatively smaller than in any other form of cat—the facial region and particularly the cranium slopes steeply downwards and gives its skull a dome-like shape.

The Cheetah's most distinctive character is the structure of its feet. Its claws are usually described as non-retractile. The claws of cats are retracted and raised from the ground by elastic ligaments which pull on the terminal joints of the toes. Now the claws of a cheetah are approximately if not quite as retractile as in some species of cats. Their distinctiveness lies in this that the claws of cats are covered in varying degrees by sheaths of skin, while the claws of a cheetah are always bared owing to the entire absence of skin sheaths.

The colour of an adult cheetah varies from tawny to a bright rufous fawn. Its coat is pale below and spotted almost everywhere with small round solid black spots. The chin and throat are buffy white, a black line runs from the corner of each eye to the upper lip, and there is a less distinct line or row of spots from the corner of the eye to below the ear. The fur is coarse; the lengthening of the hair on the neck suggests an incipient mane. A pair of cubs taken in the Berars are described as having long grey silky hair, without spots, covering the head and back and reaching half way down the flanks, giving the cub an appearance of wearing a great coat. The remainder of the body was covered with short grey hair sprinkled with single black spots. A cub taken in Nasiryah in Mesopotamia is described as being fawn-coloured—the hair on the upper part of the body was 2-3 in. long and unspotted, while the limbs and lower part of the body showed a sprinkling of dark spots. The head and body of a cheetah measures about 4-5 ft., the tail 2-5 ft., its height is from 2 ft. to 2 ft. 9 in.

We know little about the habits of the Cheetah in the wild state. In India it is usually found in low rugged hill country bordering the plains; near Hyderabad it is stated to live in holes in rocks or among accumulations of rocks and boulders. It preys on antelope, gazelle and nilgai and such creatures as it can master. One was shot in the U.P. while stalking a sambhar. Unlike other cats, speed and not stealth of movement is the essence of the Cheetah's hunting. All those characters which distinguish the Cheetah from other cats have arisen from its distinctive method of pursuing its prey. The small head, narrow chest and body, long sinewy limbs, and powerful hind quarters are designed for speed; while its protruding claws, hard, pointed pads and larger hind feet are well-fitted for securing a firm hold on hard or sandy ground. Crouching low, a cheetah takes advantage of every inch of cover or unequality in the ground till it gets within a distance to make its rush upon its quarry. While it lacks the elasticity of gait and the suppleness of body so distinctive in the cats, not the fastest antelope can equal a cheetah's initial speed. Coming up with its fleeing quarry, the Cheetah fells it by striking its hind legs from under it. The animal falls and is then seized by the throat. This manoeuvre of tripping up its prey was constantly observed in the play of a pair of cheetah cubs. The pursuer going at full speed always attempted to upset its mate by striking at the hind legs and having felled it, made for and worried it at the throat. Failing to seize its prey in its initial rush the Cheetah appears to have no reserve of strength or breath and usually gives up the chase.

Nothing is known of the breeding habits of the Cheetah in India. There is a record of female with 4 cubs which was shot near Rajkot in Central India. The mother and one cub were away when the other cubs were discovered under a bush. A pair of cubs a week old were taken in the Berars in December.

The Cheetah has been for centuries the playing thing of princes, Asiatic, African and European. When taken young it is easily tamed and trained to show its wonderful speed. A couple of cheetahs were sent as a present to Anastasius, Emperor of the East, at Constantinople in A.D. 439 from whence the sport reached Italy and obtained an enormous vogue among the wealthy, extravagant grandees of the great City States. The Turks, Moors and Persians alike used cheetahs in hunting. In India the Cheetah is usually taken blind-folded in a cart to the scene of the hunt. In the proximity of a herd of antelope it is unhooded and slipped from its leash: a short crouching stalk and a few bounds of great length and rapidity and the hunt is over—the quarry has escaped or the Cheetah holds it in a strangle-hold by the throat, till the keeper comes up and having cut the captive's throat rewards the captor with a drink of warm blood collected in its accustomed feeding bowl.

Sub-family III: *FELINAE*: TYPICAL CATS.

We have dealt with two groups of the Cat tribe, one, the *Acinonychinae*, included the Hunting Leopards, differentiated from all other cats by the absence of protective sheaths to their claws, and the other, the *Pantherinae*, comprising the Lion, Tiger, Jaguar, Leopard and Ounce, distinguished in their anatomy by the peculiar attachment of the hyoid apparatus to the cranium. It has been explained that in these Great Cats the supporting arms of the apparatus is composed partly of elastic ligament which gives greater mobility to the larynx and has its influence on the voice of these animals. The typical cats including all the smaller and medium sized forms are grouped in a third division of the tribe: the *Felinae*. In all these species the hyoid apparatus is normal. Its arms are formed of an uninterrupted chain of small bones which hold the larynx close up to the skull and restrict its movements. From this distinction in the structure of the hyoid apparatus arises those differences in the character and sonority of the voice between the great and in the lesser cats. The smaller species do not roar in the manner of lions, tigers or leopards. Apart from the roar, there is another distinctive feature about the voice of those cats in which the hyoid apparatus is normal. This is the familiar 'purr'. The great cats never purr—on the other hand, widely different species like cheetahs, pumas, lynxes and the various forms of smaller cats express pleasure and contentment by that sound.

No. 7. THE JUNGLE CAT (*FELIS CHAUS* GULD.).

The Jungle Cat has a wide distribution ranging from North Africa through Western Asia into India and Ceylon, Burma and China. The typical form of this cat, *Felis chaus chaus*, is found in the Caspian area from whence the species was originally recorded and described. Over its extensive range, 3 or 4 races of the Chaus are distinguished. The race found in India, Burma and Ceylon is known as *Felis chaus affinis*. It is said to differ from the Jungle Cats of Egypt, Palestine and the Caspian by its relatively longer tail, bright foxy red ears and slighter build. Its skull is narrower and the teeth less strongly developed. Some of the Jungle Cats from the reed beds of the River Tigris in Mesopotamia were indistinguishable from the Indian race, others approached the African form.

The Jungle Cat, the common wild cat of India, is found practically all over the Peninsula from the Himalayas to Cape Comorin. It is commoner in the drier parts of the country keeping more to grass-land and scrub-jungle and the reedy banks of rivers. In Ceylon and Burma it is again more common in the drier zones.

With its long legs and comparatively short tail—the Jungle Cat has a very distinctive appearance. Its pale green eyes give it a coldly cruel expression. The colour of its fur varies from sandy grey to yellowish grey. The tail is ringed with black towards the end and has a black tip. The paws are pale yellowish; black or sooty brown underneath. The ears are reddish, ending in a small pencil of black hairs. The underside of the body is paler with vestiges of stripes on the underside and flanks. Head and body about 2 ft. in length; tail 9 in. Weight anything from 8 to 25 lbs.

The Jungle Cat is frequently about by day—more usually in the mornings and evenings. Its movements in the open are much like those of a small panther. It preys on small mammals, birds and, when near villages, on poultry, making bold to seize its prey even in the presence of the owners. Very swift and exceedingly strong for its size, it is quite capable of bringing down larger game. Crump, writing of these cats in Kumaon says that it was not at all uncommon to find the quills of porcupines which they had killed or attempted to kill embedded in their paws.

Little definite is known about its breeding habits. Blanford states that it has two litters in a year. The kittens are easily tamed and purr like a domestic cat when pleased. They resent the approach of strangers and remain amusingly savage at feeding time.

THE DESERT CAT (*FELIS ORNATA* GRAY).

The Desert Cat is found in the desert wastes and sand hills of Sind, Cutch, Rajputana, from whence its range extends to the more arid portions of the Punjab, Kathiawar and the eastern parts of the Central Provinces.

From the structure of its skull and teeth as well as from other characters, it is deduced that our Desert Cat is the Indian representative of a group of cats, typified in Africa by the African Wild Cat, *Felis ocreata*, and in Europe by the European Wild Cat, *Felis sylvestris*. Incidentally it is interesting to mention the theory proposed by Pocock that the domestic cats found about houses and villages in India—of which there are two types, one spotted or streaked, the other uniformly grey or yellowish grey have been derived from the African Wild Cat, *Felis ocreata*, either by the introduction of tamed animals or by the reclaiming from the wild state of examples of this species which may have inhabited India in comparatively recent times. Mr. Pocock can find no evidence to support the older theory that our domestic cats have originated from indigenous Indian species such as the Chaus (*Felis chaus*) the common Jungle Cat of India, the Leopard Cat, or the Rusty Spotted Cat. It would be interesting to have authentic evidence of the inter-breeding of wild and domestic cats in India. On the other hand various so-called species of wild cats from India such as the Waved Cat (*Felis torquata*) from Nepal and Kashmir, *Felis inconspicua* from Rajputana, and *Felis huttoni* from Afghanistan are believed by Pocock to have arisen as a result of the description by different naturalists of the various colour forms of the European Wild Cat, *Felis sylvestris*, which is found in a feral state in many tropical countries.

Not much larger than a domestic cat, the Indian Desert Cat has pale yellowish fur more or less infused with grey and marked with numerous black spots. The terminal half of its tail is ringed with black. It has two horizontal stripes on its cheeks, numerous dark cross lines on the outside of the limbs and the usual two distinct black bars on the inner side of each fore-arm. The chin, throat and breast are white and unspotted. The ears are coloured like the back, with a few black hairs at the tips. It inhabits sandy plain and hills, where it preys on birds and rodents. One was killed while feeding on the carcase of a sheep. Nothing is known of its breeding habits.

THE LYNX (*LYNX LYNX* LIN.) AND THE CARACAL (*LYNX CARACAL* GULD.).

The genus Lynx includes three distinct groups of animals—the typical Lynx (*Lynx*) and its various species and races inhabiting the boreal region of North America and the cold and temperate regions of Europe and Asia, as far south as the Mediterranean and the Western Himalayas. Secondly, there are the Lynxes of the temperate region of America which range as far south as Mexico and lastly, the Caracals (*Lynx caracal*) which inhabit South-Western Asia and the greater part of Africa.

The true Lynx which occurs within our limits in the upper Indus Valley, in Gilgit, Ladak and Tibet is probably a race of the ordinary lynx of Northern Europe and Asia—distinctive in its pale sandy grey or isabelline colouring—hence its name *Lynx lynx isabellina*. It is strongly built cat of medium size with a short tail, broad head, large triangular tufted ears. Its paws are large, the claws well-sheathed, and the pads more or less concealed by hair. Its face is framed with a partial pendant ruff of long hair. In summer, its coat shows a sprinkling of spots which may persist, but usually disappear in the heavier winter coat, except on the limbs and flanks. The Lynx is a creature of high altitudes where it preys upon birds and such animals as it can kill from rodents to sheep and goats. Writers have commented upon its wild and fierce disposition. Its keen eye-sight and hearing are proverbial. Rarely seen—little is known of its habits. It is said to have 2 or 3 young—the mother usually hiding her litter in a cave or in a hole among rocks.

The Caracal (*Lynx caracal*) known as the *Siyah gosh* or 'black-eared one', is found in Sind and Cutch and is said to be common in the North and North-West Hills of the Cutch State. It is found in the drier parts of the Punjab, Rajputana, the United Provinces and Central India. Outside our limits its range extends into Persia, Mesopotamia and Arabia and over the greater part of Africa.

The Caracal has the broad head and tufted ears of a true lynx. Like the Lynx it stands higher in the hind limbs than on the fore, but it is smaller and lighter in build and has a longer tail. Its skull bears a general resemblance to that of a lynx, but is narrower in the cranial and facial portions and recalls in some of its structural characters the skull of a typical cat (*Felis*). Its coat though not as dense as that of the Lynx is yet thick and soft. The colouring is a uniform reddish grey above fading into buff or white below. Faint indications of spots are present on the under surface and sometimes on the back.

An uncommon and elusive animal, little is known about the caracal in the wild state. It is a creature of desert and scrub jungle, where it preys on birds, which it is said to take in flight by springing up at them, on rodents, antelope and small deer. There is a record of a caracal attacking a man in the Mirzapur District, U.P., but it is believed that the animal was driven to the act by hunger—it was in a very emaciated condition—or, that it made the attack in error. A captive caracal in the Mysore Zoo killed and partly ate a large cobra which had entered its cage.

Like the Cheetah, it is easily tamed and trained to show its prowess in hunting small deer, gazelle, hares and foxes and also birds such as peafowl, crane and pigeon. It relies for success upon its extraordinary agility. So perfect is the sympathy of eyes and feet, that champion performers in this sport, still popular in Persia, will kill 9 or 10 of a flock of feeding pigeons before they can leave the ground. It is interesting to note that of all the species of cats the Caracal comes nearest to the Hunting Leopard in the structure of its hind feet. It is trained to hunt in much the same way as a Cheetah, whose wide hind feet are better-fitted for securing a firm hold upon sandy ground and for traversing it more swiftly and surely than are the softer more pliable feet of other members of the cat tribe.

Nothing definite is known about the breeding habits of the animal in India. It is said to rear its young in porcupine burrows, in hollow trees or crevices among rocks—the average litter being 2-4.

PALLAS'S CAT (*TRICHAELURUS MANUL* PALL.).

Pallas's Cat is a Central Asian species. Three forms of this cat are known—the typical race is from Turkestan and Western Siberia, a second is found in Mongolia and Siberia east of Lake Baikal and the third known as *Trichaelurus manul nigripectus* Hodgs. occurs within our limits in Ladak and Tibet. Though distinguished by a number of structural peculiarities, Pallas's Cat holds in some aspects a position intermediate between the Lynxes and the true cats (*Felis*).

It is a small, long-tailed cat with a broad head, low forehead and short widely-separated ears, which appear to be set very low behind the cheeks and give the cat a strange and peculiar aspect.

Observation of the behaviour of a specimen in captivity suggested an explanation of its low forehead and the peculiar set of its ears. When watching its prey behind some rock or point of vantage—this species need not lower its ears in the accustomed manner of cats. It is able to reveal a relatively small part of its head without depressing or partially folding its ears—a habit which must to a certain extent interfere with quick hearing in other species.

The prevailing colour of the face of this cat is grey, that of the neck, back and body silvery or iron grey. The hairs on the back are sooty black at the base, then white, and again black at the tip. Traces of dark transverse stripes appear on the loins and sometimes on the limbs. The distal portion of the tail is ringed and ends in a black tip. The fur of the throat, chest, belly and thighs is considerably longer than on the flanks. It is perhaps an adaptation, which gives protection to the cat when lying or sleeping on snow-covered or frozen ground. A parallel lengthening of the hairs on the thighs and under parts of the body is seen in the Yak which, like Pallas's Cat, is a denizen of the bleak uplands of Ladak and Tibet.

Nothing is known about the habits of this cat in the wild state. It is said to live among rocks and to prey on small animals and birds. In captivity, its behaviour was distinctive from that usual in most other small felines. It showed no fear of spectators or a desire to avoid them and was very silent never uttering the familiar snarling growl or hiss. Its mew is described as recalling a 'combination of the bark of a small dog and the hoot of an owl'.

THE LEOPARD CAT (*PRIONAILURUS BENGALENSIS* KERR): THE RUSTY-SPOTTED CAT (*PRIONAILURUS RUBIGINOSUS* GEOFFR.).

The Leopard Cat was originally described from a specimen which swam on board ship in Calcutta—hence its traditional name *bengalensis*. It is found in evergreen and mixed forests practically all over India—in the Himalayas, the Eastern and Western Ghats and in South India. It is recorded from Kashmir and South Baluchistan. Eastwards from Assam its range extends through Burma and Southern China into the Malay countries.

Rounded black ears marked with a white patch on the outer surface distinguish both the Leopard Cat and the Rusty-Spotted Cat from other cats of the genus *Felis*. The Leopard Cat is about the size of a domestic cat but rather longer in the leg. Its colour and markings give it the aspect of a miniature panther. The prevailing colour of the body is yellowish above, white below, ornamented throughout with black or brownish spots. Both colour and pattern are very variable in the species, the ground colour may show a tendency to grey or rufous and the spots, usually arranged to form regular lines along the body, may coalesce into uninterrupted longitudinal bands. Among other markings are four more or less distinct bands running from the crown over the neck, which break up into short bars and elongate spots on the shoulders. There is a pair of horizontal cheek stripes, the lower joining a black bar across the throat and the usual two black bars on the inside of the fore-arm. The spots on the tail form cross bars towards its end.

This beautiful forest cat preys upon small birds and animals. It is nocturnal in habit and seldom seen. The Society's collectors found it common about villages in Coorg where it is said to be very destructive to poultry. It has 3 or 4 cubs in a litter. A kitten a month old was taken in August in the Niligiris. It became quite tame and though driven off by domestic cats returned more than once to its owners after a sojourn in the forest.

The Rusty-Spotted Cat (*Prionailurus rubiginosus*) is about half or three-quarters of the size of a domestic cat. It is a slightly built active creature with a soft, smooth, fawn grey coat, patterned with brown bars and spots arranged in more or less regular lines. The markings on its head and shoulders are dark brown; they change to rusty on the flanks and are reduced to smaller round spots on the hind quarters. The underparts are nearly white with black spots. Length of body nearly 17 in., tail half the length of the body, weight about 3 lbs. It is found in Southern India and is recorded from the hill forests of the Western Ghats at Khandala in the Poona District, and from Seoni in the Central Provinces. It is common in jungles over the whole island of Ceylon. This elegant and agile little cat lives both in forest and grasslands—in

Ceylon it is rarely seen away from jungle. It shelters by day in holes in trees or under bushes, and hunts by night preying upon small birds and mammals or on poultry, when living near villages. The female has a litter of 2-3 young and conceals them in a hollow log or tree.

THE MARBLED CAT (*PARDOFELIS MARMORATA* MARTIN).

This beautiful cat, one of the rarest of all its tribe in museum collections is found in the forests of the Eastern Himalayas and Assam from whence its range extends into Burma and the Malay countries. As a genus, the Marbled Cats are distinguished from the Leopard Cats and their oriental relatives by structural peculiarities of the skull which among other points of distinction is short and broad, more rounded and has wider cheek arches. The teeth especially the canines are relatively more robust and the chin more vertical.

Three races or forms of this cat are known. The East Himalayan race, described under the name *Pardofelis marmorata charltoni* from a specimen taken at Darjeeling, is found in Sikkim and Assam. How far this particular race extends into Burma is not known. The Himalayan Marbled Cat is said to be quite distinctive in its thicker, longer, rich ochreous brown coat whose luxuriance tends to obscure the 'marbled' pattern more apparent in typical examples from Java and Sumatra.

The general pattern on the coat of these cats consists of stripes on the crown, neck and back, of large and small blotches, making the so-called 'marbling' on the flanks and of spots on the underside of the limbs and on the tail. The marbled pattern on the flanks is variable even in cats inhabiting the same region. In the Himalayan race, it is limited to a few, wavy greyish buff stripes which break up the ground colour of the flanks into large ochreous brown patches. The heavily spotted legs are of the same rich hue as the body. The tail is darker in tone and its pattern is obscurely defined. Though much smaller in size, the Marbled Cat resembles the Clouded Leopard in colour and pattern so that young Clouded Leopards are easily confused with this species.

Nothing is known about the habits of this cat. It is conjectured that it is a purely forest cat of arboreal habit. A supposition supported by the structure of its feet which show no adaptation to ground dwelling habits. Its tree climbing and nocturnal habits are suggested as a reason for its rarity in most collections.

THE GOLDEN CAT (*PROFELIS TEMMINCKI* VIG.).

With the exception of the Clouded Leopard, the Golden Cat is the largest of the group of smaller Oriental felines (*Felinae*). It is a fine sturdily-built cat reaching nearly 5 ft. in length. The typical form of this cat (*Profelis temmincki temmincki*), distinctive in the shortness and sleekness of its coat and the absence of body markings, comes from Sumatra—from whence its range extends into the Malay Peninsula, Indo-China, Siam, Burma, Assam and the Eastern Himalayas. Golden Cats inhabiting more northern latitudes in South-Eastern Tibet, Southern and Western China are said to be distinguished by a greater luxuriance of fur; while one form from the interior of China is distinguishable by its pronounced body markings, which form bold lines and large rosettes.

The general colour of the typical Golden Cat varies from golden brown to dark brown, bright red and grey. Black examples are also known. There is usually little or no trace of pattern on the body, when the coat is short and smooth there may be a more or less distinct pattern of greyish lines on the flanks and shoulders. It is suggested that the uniform colouring of the animal without markings is a result of the enlargement and subsequent fusion of blotches and the obliteration of the paler interspaces. Kittens have longer and thicker coats than the adults but show no pattern. But whether the body pattern in the adult is retained or lost, it is always conspicuous on the face of this cat giving it a very striking aspect. Most conspicuous is a horizontal white or buff cheek stripe, sometimes edged with black running from below the eye to behind the gape. On the inner side of the eye there is always a whitish stripe which bifurcates above and is continuous with a more or less distinct greyish stripe passing on to the crown. Occasionally there are curved lines running back from above the eye to between the ears.

Nothing definite is known about the habits of this cat. The Mishmis say that it breeds in hollow trees and has two young. The Lushai hunters state that it lives among rocks and does not climb trees. There is however a record of one which took refuge in a tree from a dog. It did not display the fierceness usually ascribed to this species, which in Burma is known as *Kya Min*, signifying that it dominates other cats even tigers!

The Golden Cat preys on poultry, sheep and goats and small deer. One was shot near Maymyo on a calf that it had killed; another was speared at Victoria Point, Mergui, after killing a buffalo calf.

THE FISHING CAT (*PRIONAILURUS* OR *ZIBETHAILURUS VIVERRINUS* BENNETT).

The Fishing Cat inhabits forest and swamps at the base of the Himalayas as far west as Nepal. It is found in parts of Bengal, the United Provinces and Sind. It is unknown from the Peninsula of India except in the creeks and backwaters of the Malabar Coast between Mangalore and Cape Comorin. It is found sparingly in the jungles of Ceylon, except perhaps in the dry Northern Zone—in the wetter parts of Burma and Tenasserim, in Southern China and Formosa.

The body of a large fishing cat measures about 2 ft. 6 in. and its tail is about a foot in length. It scales nearly 25 lbs. Short in limb and rather stout in build, its body is covered with short coarse, earthy grey fur, infused with brown. The body markings consist of a series of elongate spots arranged in more or less longitudinal rows. They vary in size and sharpness of definition in individuals. From 6 to 8 dark lines run from the forehead over the crown on to the neck breaking up into shorter bars and spots on the shoulders. The cheeks are greyish white with two usually well-defined horizontal black or brown stripes. Markings on the limbs are indistinct or wanting. The two usual dark bars appear on the inside of the fore-arm. The lower parts of the body are spotted and the tail is more or less distinctly ringed with black.

The Fishing Cat lives in heavy jungle, or in scrub, frequently in grass swamps or in reed beds, about rivers and tidal creeks. It preys on any animal and bird that it can secure and has been known to kill calves and sheep, to carry off dogs and even children. There is the record of a newly-caught male which killed a leopardess twice its size after breaking through the partition which separated their cages. It is given to feeding on fish and fresh water molluscs. Its method of fishing is to crouch on a rock or overhanging bank and to scoop up the fish with a blow of its paw. It does not enter the water in pursuit of its prey. The fore-feet of this cat have moderately well-developed webs between the toes, the claw sheaths are not large enough to completely envelope the retracted claws, the ends of which project considerably beyond the sheaths.

Nothing is known about the breeding habits of this cat. A single kitten was taken from a lair consisting of a beaten down patch among reeds with runs leading to it from opposite sides.

THE CLOUDED LEOPARD (*NEOFELIS NEBULOSA* GRIFFITH).

The Clouded Leopard is found in the forests of Sikkim, Bhutan, in Assam, in the dense evergreen forests in the extreme north and south of Burma, in Siam, the Malay Peninsula and Borneo.

The size of a Clouded Leopard is that of a small panther. A large male measured 6½ ft.; 3 ft. of which consisted of tail. The animal has a long body and tail and short limbs and rounded black ears relieved by a greyish patch in the centre. The structure of its feet is much like that of the panther and its near relatives, the tiger and lion. From the panther it differs in the structure of the hyoid apparatus and in peculiarities in the structure of the skull and the set of the teeth. Very striking is the Clouded Leopard in the enormous relative development of the upper canine teeth, which present the nearest approach among living cats to the great tusks of the extinct sabre-toothed tiger.

The markings of the Clouded Leopard give it a beauty and distinction equalled by a few of its tribe. The general colour of the body varies from grey or earthy brown to pale or rich yellowish brown fading to white or pale tawny on the under-parts. The face is marked with the usual cheek stripes so common in the smaller cats, and the head is spotted. Two broad bands, with narrower bands or elongate spots between them run from between the ears to the shoulders and extend more or less regularly in the form of large oval or elongate marks on the back. The clouded pattern of the flanks is formed by dark blotches more or less lined with black and divided by paler interspaces. The limbs and under-parts are marked with large spots and the tail ornamented with rings frequently imperfect on the sides.

Little is recorded about the habits of this beautiful animal. It is said to be strictly arboreal in habit and to prey on animals and birds after the manner of its kind. There is a record of one which was killed while advancing to attack a herd boy who split its skull with his *dah*.

FAMILY: II. *VIVERRIDAE*: CIVETS, GENETS, ETC.

The family includes the True Civets and their numerous relatives—Genets, Palm Civets, Lisangs, Bear Cats. They form a diverse assemblage of animals, which in certain characters connected with the structure of the skull and the anatomy of the body display some affinity to the Cats (*Felidæ*) and, they are generally regarded as their next of kin. Nevertheless the Civets do not reveal that uniformity in build which is so distinctive of the Cat Tribe. Marked structural differences among them make it difficult to provide a general definition which would distinguish them as a tribe from other beasts of prey. They differ from cats in many ways. None of the civets attain the size of the great cats, they are all comparatively small creatures, long in body, short in limb with elongated heads and pointed muzzles. We have seen how the teeth of cats show a marked adaptation to a purely carnivorous diet; how specialization to this end is revealed in a shortening and strengthening of the jaws, in a marked development of the canine teeth and in a reduction in the number of molar teeth, whose blade like crowns make them perfect cutting instruments. The jaws of civets on the other hand show no reduction in the length and carry almost the full number of teeth of a typical carnivore. They have a larger number of cheek teeth than any of the existing cats.

All the Indian members of the tribe have four premolar teeth on each side of the upper and lower jaws and one or more true molars. The canine teeth are more feeble than those of cats, the flesh-tooth is less trenchant and more tubercular in character. The long pointed cusps of the cheek teeth of some of the *Viverridae* recall the dentition of an insectivorous animal; while the molars of others, like the Palm Civets and the Bear Cat, which feed largely on fruit, have almost lost their carnivorous character. The teeth of civets help to show how, within the limits of a single family, while the family characters of the dentition may be retained, the form and size of the teeth may vary in accordance with the habits of life and the food of the individual species.

In the structure of the feet again the civets display a lesser degree of specialization than the cats. The number of toes both in the fore and hind feet is generally five. This is seen in all the Indian members of the tribe, whereas cats have five toes in the fore foot and four in the hind. The claws vary in retractability. In some forms, as in the True Civets (*Viverra*), some of the claws of the fore feet are as retractile and as well protected by sheaths as in many species of cats. In other forms this character is less apparent. Yet another point of distinction in civets is the entire absence of the sharp pointed conical papillae which convert a cat's tongue into a rasp.

It will be seen that while the civets display some affinity to the cats, their general equipment as beasts of prey places them on a lower level. They display in their build and their armament of teeth and claws a lower degree of adaptation to carnivorous habits of life.

No representative of the family exists in America or Australia. All its members are confined to the warmer parts of the Old World, chiefly to Africa, Madagascar and South-Eastern Asia. One species is found in Southern Europe.

Pocock in his classification of the family recognises a number of groups or sub-families. The following occur in our area:

Sub-family	*Viverrinae*:	True Civets.
,,	*Paradoxurinae*:	Palm Civets.
,,	*Prionodontinae*:	Tiger Civets or Lisangs.
,,	*Arctogalidinae*:	Small Toothed Palm Civets.
,,	*Hemigalinae*:	Banded Civets.

Sub-family: 1. *VIVERRINAE.*

True Civets.

The Civet tribe (*Viverridae*) has been differently classified by various naturalists. Pocock in his recent classification limits the sub-family *Viverrinae*, which includes the true or typical Civets, to five genera. They are as follows: The Large Oriental Civets of the genus *Viverra;* a second genus *Moschothera*, formed to distinguish two large civets, one found in Malabar, the other in Lower Burma and the adjoining Malay countries; the small civets of the genus *Viverricula;* and finally the two African genera *Civettictis* and *Genetta.*

Apart from the Genets which are found also in Southern Europe, the True Civets are confined entirely to the Oriental and Ethiopian region.

The *Viverrinae* or True Civets form a compact little group, distinguished from the Palm Civets or Paradoxures by the form of their feet and the more elaborate structure of their scent pouches.

In these True Civets, the plantar or central pad under the fore foot is reduced in size and, compared with the Palm Civets, there is an even greater reduction in the size of the carpal pad (a small pad in the region of the wrist). On the hind foot the corresponding pad is almost or entirely suppressed. Further in the True Civets the whole under-surface of the foot with the exception of the pads is almost completely covered with hair. The growth of hair under the feet, the reduction or suppression of the carpal and plantar pads is variable in different members of the group. But on the whole these characters, which are more or less marked in True Civets, indicate a greater adaptation in these animals to a terrestrial life. Palm Civets, on the other hand, are mainly tree-dwelling animals. Their naked soles and well developed pads fit them in a greater degree for an arboreal existence.

Like cats, true civets walk upon their toes, and their feet bear a close superficial resemblance to the digitigrade feet of cats. This resemblance is seen particularly in the reduction of the carpal pads and in the hairiness of the under foot. The resemblance is carried further in certain members of the group such as the Small Civets (*Viverricula*) whose feet are perhaps the most feline in character. In these little civets, as in cats, the hallux and pollex, or those digits which correspond to the thumb and big toe, are placed high up on the foot and at some distance from the other digits. Again in the large civets of the genus *Viverra* some of the claws of the fore feet are protected with sheaths of hairy skin. These claws are therefore as retractile as those of many species of cats. As we have already seen, the extent to which different species of cats can sheath their claws varies considerably.

The true civets have well developed scent glands. They produce the well known perfume which gives the name to the tribe. The word 'civet' is derived from the Arabic term *zabat*, a name used for the scent derived from the glands of these animals. The structure of these glands varies in different members of the group. It may even differ to some extent in males and females of the same species. These glands generally take the form of two elongate eminences covered internally and externally with hair. They are found in both sexes and lie just in front of the testes in the male and in a corresponding position in the female. In Genets the two lobes of this gland lie closely apposed. Their line of contact is marked with a Y-shaped groove. When pulled apart the space between the glands will be found to consist of three compartments separated by folds of skin. The secretion of the glands exudes into these compartments from clusters of tiny pores in the lateral walls. In the large Oriental Civets (*Viverra*), the glandular space between the lobes is not divided into compartments. Nor are the two lobes of the gland closely apposed through their entire length. In their posterior half towards the scrotum the two glands are somewhat widely separated, but anteriorly their inner margins fuse together to form the roof of a deep pouch, which constitutes a large storage chamber for the secretion of the glands. In a male of the large civet (*V. zibetha*) examined by Pocock the naked skin between the testes was found to be glandular as also a thick fold of integument which almost completely encircles the anus. The secretion from the gland surrounding the anus has however a very different and extremely offensive odour. The secretion from the perfume gland is used both for perfumery and for medicinal purposes. In India it is held to have valuable medicinal and aphrodisiac properties. The secretion contains free ammonia, resin, fat, and a volatile oil to which its ordoriferous properties are due. It is a strong smelling perfume and requires a highly trained nose for its appreciation. The so-called 'civet' perfume of commerce which is imported into India, comes from America. It is not obtained from civets, but is taken from the Beaver.

In India the secretion is collected from the Large Indian Civet (*V. zibetha*) and to a greater extent from the Small Civet (*V. indica*). It is much sought after by some of the Brahmins of Malabar and as much as Rs. 10 per tola is paid for the pure essence. The 'civet' obtainable in the bazaars is much adulterated with butter and oil to increase its weight. The best prices are paid for the entire pouch cut from a freshly killed animal. The usual method of collecting 'civet' is to scrape it out of the animal's scent pouch with a wooden spoon. It is recorded that there was an establishment once maintained at the expense of the Travancore Government in which civets were reared for the purpose of collecting the perfume. Numbers of Small Indian Civets are still kept at Kolar in East Mysore for the same purpose. 'Civet' is very largely produced in Java from the Javanese race of the animal (*V. indica rasse*), where it is used very considerably for flavouring tobacco smoked by the Javanese.

THE LARGE INDIAN CIVET (*VIVERRA ZIBETHA* LINN.).

This Large Civet is found from North India and Northern China through Burma, Siam and the Malay Peninsula.

It is a sturdily built animal with a long head, long flattened body, stumpy legs and small rounded feet—a build, typical of the true civets. An adult animal measures nearly 4 feet in length: its thick tapering tail is more than half as long as the head and body.

The general colouration is a dark hoary grey, frequently washed yellowish or brown. An erectile crest of long deep black hairs runs down the middle of the back. The crest is distinctive and differentiates the Large Civets from the Small Civets of the genus *Viverricula*. The crest forms a heavy black stripe from the shoulders to the first ring of the tail. The tail is completely ringed with six broad black bands. Pale bands form an edging to the black dorsal crest. There are several dark bands on the chest and shoulders. The sides of the body are either plain or have more or less distinct markings. Such markings may be obscured or obliterated in the longer and more luxuriant winter coat. A seasonal change of coat takes place between May and July. It is more marked in animals inhabiting the northern areas of the civets range.

The luxuriance or otherwise of the winter coat and the prominence of pattern are some of the characters which are used to differentiate between the various races of this animal. The typical race (*V. z. zibetha*) is found in Nepal, Sikkim and Northern Bengal. Compared with the Chinese race (*V. z. ashtoni*), it has a moderately long winter coat. The race from Burma and Assam is *V. z. picta*. It is said to be distinguishable by the persistence of pattern even in the winter coat. A third race, *V. z. pruinosa* is found in Tenasserim and the Malay Peninsula. It is distinguished from the more northern races by the shortness of the coat and distinctness of its pattern in the winter months, seasonal variation in coat in this race is very slight. A fourth race *V. z. surdaster* is described from Indo-China.

The Large Indian Civet is a solitary creature sheltering in bushes, thick grass or heavy scrub jungle by day, and coming out to hunt by night. It preys on small animals and birds and may be very destructive to poultry. Like most carnivores, it feeds on anything worth killing and its food may include, snakes, frogs, fishes, crabs and even insects. It is not exclusively carnivorous, and feeds equally on fruits and certain roots. It takes readily to water. It breeds in May and June, and usually has four or five young. The scent glands, are large, measuring, when dissected out, about 2.5 inches in length and 1.5 in. in breadth. Dogs are said to be greatly excited by the scent of this civet and will leave that of any other animal for it.

In addition to the Large Indian Civet (*V. zibetha*), two other large species are found in our area. They are the Large Malabar Civet (*Moschothera civettina*) found in Travancore and Cochin, and the Burmese Civet (*M. megaspila*) which is found in Southern Burma, Siam, Annam, Cochin China and the Malay Peninsula. These two civets, now regarded as representing a distinct genus, differ from the Large Civets of the genus *Viverra* by the absence of sheaths to the claws of the fore feet, and by the comparatively hairless condition of the skin between the pads of the feet. Both species are very rare. The general colouration and markings are very similar to the Large Indian Civet, except that the white bands on the tail do not completely encircle it. The general habit of these civets are similar to those of the Large Indian Civet.

THE SMALL INDIAN CIVET (*VIVERRICULA INDICA*, GEOFFROY).

The Small Civet is found in the Peninsula of India, from Sind, the Punjab and the foot hills of the Himalayas, southwards to Ceylon and eastwards through Burma into Southern China, Indo-China, Annam, Burma, Malacca and Java.

The absence of a dorsal crest of long black hairs will serve to distinguish this civet from the large civets of the genus *Viverra*. It is a much smaller animal. A well grown adult male is a slightly over 3 feet in entire length, the tail being a little over a foot long. It scales from 6-8 lbs.

The general colouration of a typical specimen from Southern India varies from brownish or olivaceous grey to light grey. There are longitudinal dark stripes and rows of spots along the body, a stripe down each side of the neck and frequently one across the throat. The tail is ringed with grey and brown. The under-fur is brownish or greyish and varies in density. Before the moult the coat becomes hard, brittle and lustreless. The change to the fuller winter coat takes place after September.

Various Indian races of this civet are now recognised. The distinctions between these forms are based on colouration, size, cranial and other characters. The typical race (*V. indica indica*) is said to inhabit Southern India from the Western Ghats across the peninsula to the Eastern Ghats as far as the Chilka lake in Orissa. A second race, *V. i. bengalensis* is apparently found in the central portion of India, south of the Ganges, from Calcutta to Gujerat and possibly in Sind. More or less distinct races are said to occur also in the following areas: *V. i. deserti* (Rajputana); *V. i. wellsi* (Punjab and the United Provinces); *V. i. baptistae* (from Bhutan, Upper Bengal, Assam); *V. i. thai* (from Siam and Indo-China and probably also in Upper Burma); *V. i. klossi* (in the Malay Peninsula and apparently in Lower Burma); *V. i. mayori* (in Ceylon). A detailed description of these races will be found in Pocock's monograph on the 'Civet Cats of Asia' published in the *Journal of the Bombay Natural History Society* (vol. xxxvi, p. 647).

The Small Indian Civet is a shy seclusive animal, almost entirely nocturnal in its habits. It lives in holes in the ground or under rocks or thick bushes. It is frequently found in the neighbourhood of villages or even within the large towns. It climbs well and will scale a vertical tree trunk with ease. It is more arboreal in habit than is usual with the true civets. Though it kills poultry when opportunity offers, like other civets, it prefers preying on rats, lizards, small birds and insects. It feeds on fruit and is fond of the berries of the Ber (*Zizyphus jujuba*). It is easily tamed. The species is frequently kept under domestication for collecting the secretion of its scent glands.

Sub-family: 2. *PARADOXURINAE.*

Palm Civets.

The Civet Tribe (*Viverridae*) contains a second group of animals —the *Paradoxurinae* of which the Palm Civets or Toddy Cats are the dominant members. This group also includes the Binturong or Bear Cat (*Arctictis*) and a rare genus of civet from the Celebes (*Macrogalida*).

External characters which distinguish the Palm Civets from the true civets are seen in the form of the limbs. The Palm Civets are short-legged animals. Unlike true civets, they walk to a greater extent upon the soles of their feet. Again in distinction to the true civets, the soles of the feet, both in the fore and hind limbs, are almost completely naked. Further the greater development of the pads which lie behind the central or plantar pad of the foot indicates a more perfect adaptation in these animals to an arboreal existence than is revealed in the true civets.

The perfume glands are also very different from those of the true civets. The plan of their structure is much less elaborate. The secretion of the glands is discharged into a slight fold of skin instead of a deep pouch. There is a large area of naked skin, corresponding to the glands in front of the scrotum in the males and around the genito-urinary orifice in the females. The secretion from the anal gland in some forms is singularly fetid and can be discharged under stress of fear or excitement. The teeth vary very much in development and are very large in some species while they are small in others. They are suited to the mastication of both animal and vegetable food.

The Palm Civets are comprised in two genera, *Paradoxurus* and *Paguma*, which are distinguished by characters of the skull. These animals are exclusively Asiatic, ranging from India, Burma, through the Malayan Region to the South of China. They also occur in the Philippines, Celebes and Formosa.

THE COMMON PALM CIVET OR TODDY CAT (*PARADOXURUS HERMAPHRODITUS* GRAY).

The best known of all the Palm Civets is the Common Palm Civet or Toddy Cat (*Paradoxurus hermaphroditus*). It is found in Ceylon and practically over the whole of India from the Himalayas to Cape Comorin. Eastwards its range extends through Assam and Burma to South China and the Malay countries and Islands as far east as the Philippines, Borneo and the Moluccas. Blanford in his *Mammals of India* applied the name *niger*, to the Indian Palm Civet and the name *hermaphroditus* to the Malayan species. Pocock in his recent review of the species recognises but one species as inhabiting India and South-Eastern Asia, and considers the name *hermaphroditus* as more correctly applicable to it.

The tail of the Common Palm Civet is nearly or quite as long as its head and body which may be slightly over 2 feet in length. Its weight averages from 6 to 9 lbs.

The general colour of its coarse, somewhat ragged fur is black, blackish or brownish grey, the shorter grey or brown under fur of the coat, when present, is partly or wholly concealed by overlying longer and darker hairs. These longer hairs are generally paler towards the tips and as such hardly distinguishable in colour from the pale under wool. But in certain areas of the body the long hairs of the coat are dark throughout. These dark areas by contrast with the paler surrounding hair tend to suggest a pattern of black stripes on the back. A similar suggestion of spots is seen in the flanks and sometimes on the thighs and shoulders. This pattern is not always obvious. It is generally most prominent in an animal which has freshly moulted its hair. The season of coat change varies in different localities. Generally, the civets are in poor coat between May and October, and in full coat between December and March. The change of coat naturally makes a profound change in the general appearance of the animal. It is more marked in some localities and less appreciable in others. The luxuriance of the coat, the extent of development of the under fur, the obviousness or otherwise of the pattern, the comparative size of the teeth, minor distinctions in the skull have been used as characters to distinguish between the numerous races of the civet. The typical form is said to occur in Central and Southern India and Ceylon.

The Civet is generally known in India as the Toddy Cat, because of its habit of climbing Palmyra palms to drink the toddy which flows into the jars hung up by the toddy-drawers. In Java the species is known as the 'Coffee Cat', owing to its habit of collecting in numbers round coffee plantations to feed on the ripe berries. The seeds of the berries are passed out whole by the animal, generally on a pathway or against the stumps of trees. They are subsequently collected by the coffee gatherers when the regular picking is over. Palm Civets appear to be largely frugivorous, though like other civets, they feed on small animals, birds and insects. They are arboreal and rest by day concealed among the branches of a tree or curled up in a hole in the trunk. They are common round villages and have even been found in the centre of towns and cities. They usually select to live in the rafters of houses, or in drains and come out at night in quest for food. When taken young this civet is easily tamed and in confinement eats cooked food of almost any kind. The animal probably breeds throughout the year. The majority have their young after the rains, during the cold weather, 4-6 young are born at a time.

A second species of Palm Civet, the Brown Palm Civet (*P. jerdoni*), is found in the hill ranges of Southern India. It is distinguishable from the Common Palm Civet by its rich deep brown colouring, the back and flanks are somewhat grizzled. The vibrissae (whiskers) are dark brown. Unlike the Common Palm Civet the hair on the neck of this civet is reversed and its growth is directed forwards towards the head. Its habits are similar to the Common Palm Civet.

THE CHINESE PALM CIVET (*PAGUMA LARVATA* GRAY).

The genus *Paguma* is now considered to include but two species of Palm Civet, the Tibetan Palm Civet (*P. lanigera*), about which little is known, and the Chinese Palm Civet (*P. larvata*). The Himalayan Palm Civet (*P. grayi*) and the Sumatran Palm Civet (*P. leucomystax*) are now looked upon merely as racial forms of the Chinese Palm Civet whose range extends from Southern China to the Himalayas as far west as Kashmir and reaches southwards through Burma to the Andaman Islands, Sumatra and Borneo.

The Chinese Palm Civet (*P. larvata*) is distinguished from the Common Palm Civet (*Paradoxurus*) by certain characters of the skull. Its skull is more robust, has a broader waist, and the bony palate extends well beyond the molar teeth of the upper jaw. From differences in the muscularity of the skull and the less trenchant character of its teeth it is inferred that *Paguma* is less predatory and more of a vegetable feeder than *Paradoxurus*.

Externally, the Chinese Palm Civet may be distinguished by its white whiskers and by the entire absence of any suggestion of spots or stripes on its body. The general colouring ranges from grey to tawny. The lower parts are paler or whitish. The under fur is brownish, grey or dusky. Markings more or less obvious are present on the face. More or less distinctive is a fringe of white hairs in front of the ears which projects over the cheeks. A line running down the middle from the forehead to the nose, and a blotch or spot below each eye usually stand out as markings from a more conspicuous intermingling of white hairs. The whiskers are mostly white. In a male and female of this species captured in Almora District, United Provinces, the male appeared to be altogether darker in general colouration. Its facial markings were less pronounced—more grizzled—the darker hairs predominating. The facial markings of the female were on the other hand more distinct and stood out more clearly from a predominance of white hairs in the markings. How far this differentiation in the colouring of the sexes is prevalent remains to be ascertained. There is much individual variation in the facial markings. They may be well emphasised or indistinct, the nape of the neck may be pale or dark brown or black or conspicuously speckled with grey. Variation is also seen in the development of the fringe of hairs in front of the ears and in the length of the winter coat. These variations may be to some extent correlated with certain areas of the animals' distribution and are used to distinguish various geographical races of this civet. Six races are recognised as occurring in the Indian Empire. Descriptions indicating the distinctive characters of these races will be found in the *Journal of the Bombay Natural History Society* (vol. xxxvii, p. 326).

As regards size, the Himalayan forms stand midway between the small Chinese race and the large Malayan races. An adult male from Kumaon measured a little short of 4 ft. 2 in. in total length of which 2 ft. was tail. Its weight was 11½ lbs.

The habits of this Palm Civet are very similar to those of the Common Palm Civet. It is perhaps more frugivorous—though, like all civets it subsists also on animal food, eating anything which it can kill. It is a creature of mountain forests, living and breeding in holes in trees. Four young were found on one occasion. It is easily tamed and in captivity is described as being of 'cleanly habits, without the unpleasant odour usually emitted by civets'. But when irritated this civet is known to discharge a thin, most fetid yellow fluid from its anal glands. It is probable that the Common Palm Civet shares this habit which is obviously a means of defence. The prominent white vibrissae (whiskers) are highly sensitive and apparently used in some way to ascertain the nature of the food. They are very mobile, and are projected forwards or switched back in the direction of the cheeks. It was observed in the case of a captive pair that fruit, when presented to them, was always first touched with the tips of the projected whiskers before it was accepted. The female when given an apple usually took it in her fore paws and, squatting on her haunches, ate it in the manner of a squirrel eating a nut. This particular pair of civets were caught in a trap baited with ripe tomatoes. They had eaten about fifty of these fruits from a tray left out the night before.

THE BINTURONG OR BEAR CAT (*ARCTICTIS BINTURONG* RAFFLES).

The Binturong is easily distinguished from other civets. The back of its ears is clothed with tufts of long hairs, while its long coarse shaggy coat is suggestive of a bear's. Its tail is long and prehensile, very thick at the root, tapering gradually, and covered with bristly straggling hairs longer than those on the body. The soles of its hind feet are naked to the heel. In these characters the Binturong differs from its relatives the Palm Civets. Nevertheless it reveals a resemblance to them in the structure of the scent glands and in the fusion of the pads of the third and fourth toes of its hind feet.

This civet is found in Nepal, Sikhim, Bhutan, Assam, Upper Burma and Indo-China from thence its range extends southward through Arrakan, Tenasserim, Sumatra, Java and Borneo.

The general colouring of the animal is black. The hair of the face, the limbs, the nape, flank and rump may be tipped or 'ringed' with grey, tawny or foxy red. When profuse the variation may reduce the dominant colouring from black to grey or tawny. This is particularly noticeable in animals from India, Burma and Indo-China, which are regarded as a distinct race (*A. b. albifrons*). These northern animals are also characterised by the length and luxuriance of their winter coats. In the typical race, which inhabits Tenasserim and the Malay Peninsula, the winter coat is shorter and the general colour consistently darker, the long hairs never being profusely anulated. The skull, as compared with that of the northern form, is larger and more massive. A large Binturong from Siam had a total length of 66 in. of which 34 in. was the head and body measurement, 32 in. the tail. Recorded weights vary from 13 to 25½ lbs.

The Binturong lives in dense forests. Owing to its seclusive nocturnal habits, it is seldom seen and is therefore comparatively rare in Museum collections. Like other civets, it is carnivorous, feeding on small animals, birds, fishes, earthworms. It also eats fruit. It is arboreal in habit and uses its prehensile tail as an aid in climbing. It is the only placental mammal in the Old World with a truly prehensile tail. Its ability to support itself by its tail has been doubted, but it has been observed that the young at any rate can support themselves by the extremity of the tail alone.

Nothing is known about the breeding habits of this animal.

Sub-family: 3. *PRIONODONTINAE.*

The Tiger Civets or Lisangs.

THE SPOTTED TIGER CIVET (*PRIONODON PARDICOLOR* HODGSON).

The beautiful Tiger Civets or Lisangs are now grouped in a sub-division of the tribe—the *Prionodontinae.* They are distinguished from the rest of the Oriental Civets by the absence of scent glands in both sexes, by a characteristic configuration of the genital organs and by the highly specialised character of their teeth. Instead of forty teeth as found in the true civets, they have only thirty-eight. The second upper molar is usually absent or, if present, it is rudimentary. The teeth are sharp and compressed. They indicate that the diet of these animals is carnivorous. They probably feed to some extent on insects also. Their feet differ from those of the Palm Civets (*Paradoxurus* and *Paguma*) in the hairiness of the areas round the pads, and, in this particular, they resemble the true civets (*Viverra*). Their claws are sheathed and therefore completely retractile.

In the absence of scent glands, in the posterior position of the external genitals, in the hairy soled feet and sharp retractile claws, the Tiger Civets show a remarkable combination of feline characters. Even the teeth with their trenchant blades and in their numerical reduction foreshadow the characteristic dentition of cats. Nevertheless the long slender muzzled skull, bodily form and the arrangement of the pads of the feet of the Lisangs essentially class them as civets.

Two species are known. The Spotted Tiger Civet (*Prionodon pardicolor*) and the Banded Tiger Civet (*P. lisang*). Both animals are graceful and delicate in build, sinuous and slender in body, long in the muzzle and very long in the tail. The striking colouration has suggested the name Tiger Civet. The band-like markings of one and the spots of the other differentiate the two species externally.

The Spotted Tiger Civet (*P. pardicolor*) inhabits Nepal, Sikhim, Assam and extends its distribution into Upper Burma and Indo-China. The general colouring ranges from dusky brown to bright buff. The markings consist of two long stripes extending from behind the ears to the shoulders or beyond and of a stripe on each side of the neck. Along the back there are usually two rows of small spinal spots which may coalesce posteriorly to form a stripe. The central row of body markings is flanked on either side with three or four rows of large spots which cover the shoulders, flanks and thighs. The fore legs are spotted to the paws; the hind legs to the thighs, and the tail has about nine complete rings. Animals from Nepal and Sikhim, are distinguished by their darker colouring and generally bolder pattern. The spots are large and symmetrically arranged. They are regarded as representing the typical race which intergrades with the more easterly form, *P. pardicolor persina,* which is generally lighter in hue and has smaller, more oval, less lineally arranged spots.

The Banded Lisang (*P. lisang*) is found in Tenasserim, and the Malay Peninsula, Sumatra, Java, Borneo. It possibly extends its range northwards into Siam. In this species the spots on the body are fused to form six broad longitudinal bands.

The Spotted Tiger Civet hunts in trees or on the ground. It lives and breeds in hollows of decayed trees and preys on small birds and animals. The time of breeding is said to be between February and August and the litter to consist of two young—there being two litters in each year. A tame specimen kept by Hodgson was 'wonderfully docile and tractable, very sensitive to cold and very fond of being petted'. It was fed on raw meat and refused fish or eggs. It was perfectly free from odour.

Sub-family: 4. *ARCTOGALIDINAE.*

The Small-toothed Palm Civets.

THE WHITE-EARED PALM CIVET (*ARCTOGALIDIA LEUCOTIS* BLYTH).

The Small-toothed Palm Civets (*Arctogalidia*) are now recognised as representing a small distinctive group or sub-family.

Externally they are distinguished from all other civets by the absence of perfume glands in the male, which has no naked glandular area in front of the scrotum. In the female the gland is represented externally by two low ridges of naked skin capable of being folded over in front of the generative orifice and continuous behind on each side with the naked area which surrounds it. The feet of these civets resemble those of the Paradoxures except that the pads of the third and fourth digits of the hind foot are not fused and the carpal or wrist pads of the fore feet are relatively longer. The surface of all the foot pads is smooth and not granular as in *Paradoxurus*. As implied by the name the small-toothed civets are distinguished by their relatively small cheek teeth.

In bodily form and in length of limb and tail, the small-toothed civets resemble the Common Palm Civet. But the markings when present are different. They are limited at most to three dark bands along the back. These may be continuous or broken up into spots. Two species are known, one of which, the White-eared Palm Civet occurs within our area. It ranges from Assam to Laos, southwards through Burma and Western Siam to Tenasserim, the Mergui Archipelago and the Islands of the North-West Coast of the Malay Peninsula. Within this range three forms are recognised. The typical form, *A. leucotis leucotis* is found in Southern Burma, Arrakan, Western Siam, Tenasserim and the Mergui Archipelago. The general colour of its fur ranges from dusky grey to bright tawny. The terminal portion of the back of the ears is covered more or less with white hair, the head is usually darker, the muzzle, paws and the distal portion of the tail brownish, the underside is usually greyish white or creamy buff. A white or creamy patch is usually distinguishable on the chest. There is a white streak on the nose and lower forehead and three blackish or brownish stripes along the back. They are sometimes traceable on the neck. The median stripe is distinct; the lateral more or less broken up into spots, less defined and sometimes absent. Transverse stripes or rings are more or less discernible on the basal and mid region of the tail. In animals inhabiting Assam the more northerly areas of the range the dorsal stripes are wide, black and all equally conspicuous. They are consigned to a second race (*A. l. millsi*). A third smaller form *A. l. macra* is said to occur in Dome Island and possibly in the small islands of the north-west coast of the Malay Peninsula.

The second species *A. trivirgata* ranges from Peninsular Siam to Borneo. In this species the ears not parti-coloured the whole outer surface of the ear is clothed with black hairs and the skin is similarly pigmented.

The White-eared Palm Civet is thoroughly arboreal in habit, numbers of them were shot on trees round Tenasserim village. The stomach of one contained the remains of squirrels. Though no doubt partly frugivorous, all the Palm Civets in the Tenasserim area live largely on squirrels and they are a considerable factor in keeping down the numbers of these animals, which are so destructive in the coconut plantations.

Sub-family: 5. *HEMIGALINAE*.

The Hemigales.

THE BANDED PALM CIVET (*HEMIGALUS DERBYANUS*).

The Hemigales resemble the true civets (*Viverrinae*) in having scent glands which are present in both sexes. They are less elaborate 'consisting of an elongated pouch with thickened hairy labia situated a little in front of the scrotum in the male, but not extending as far as the base of the penis. In the female the scent glands are situated near the anus and in the vicinity of the vagina. The feet of the Hemigales are intermediate in structure between those of the digitigrade *Viverrinae* and the plantigrade *Paradoxurinae*.

Three genera are included in this group one of which, i.e., the Banded Palm Civet (*Hemigalus derbyanus*) occurs in our area only in Tenasserim from whence its range extends through the Malay Peninsula to Sumatra and Borneo.

The animal is about the size of a Common Palm Civet. It has short close fur of a buffy grey colour. The general colouring of the body is largely determined by the colour of the under-wool and the extent to which it is exposed or covered by the longer hairs. The colour of the under-wool ranges from varying shades of buff to bright orange buff, the longer hairs except on the bands are partly whitish, greyish or buffy. The markings are very distinctive. A longitudinal stripe runs from each ear backwards to meet a broad transverse band across the shoulder. Behind these are four or five broad transverse black stripes on the back, the tail is also banded with black. The dorsal bands are very variable in shape and width and in the extent to which they break up on the flanks.

The species is by no means common. It is said to have absolutely no smell—it is very active and probably largely arboreal. A specimen caught alive was very savage and growled like a wild cat.

FAMILY: III. *HERPESTIDAE*: MUNGOOSES.

The Mungooses are usually classified as one of the primary sub-divisions of the Civet Tribe. Pocock in a recent study of the group finds a number of positive and negative characters in these animals which he considers sufficient to differentiate them from the Civets and give them the status of a distinct tribe or family. Among the characters which distinguish Mungooses from Civets is the complete absence of perfume glands in both sexes. The absence of these glands in the Mungoose results in a distinctive configuration of the external genital organs. Differences are also seen in the structure of the feet and the ears.

With the exception of one African genus, the ears of mungooses are more or less semicircular in shape and so small that their upper margins do not project above the head or the nape. The structure of the external ear reveals a series of complicated folds which can be shut down one over the other so as to completely close its cavity. This development is not seen in the Civets, animals usually living on the ground or in trees. Mungooses on the other hand frequently live in burrows of their own making, and the complicated mechanism for closing the cavity of the ear is believed to be a special development for excluding dust or dirt when burrowing.

The feet of mungooses are armed with comparatively long or very long claws. They are better developed in the fore feet. The terminal joints of the toes are not provided with ligaments for raising the claws off the ground, nor are the claws furnished with protective sheaths of skin and hence they are always bared. The feet of mungooses however display a wide range of variation. In the standard pattern of foot possessed by many genera, including our Common Mungoose (*Herpestes*), there are 5 toes. The four main digits are well developed but those which correspond to the thumb and the big toe are small, and in some African species these digits disappear altogether, either in the hind foot alone, or both in the hind and fore feet. The four main toes are united with webs—the presence, or the depth of the webs vary in different species. The soles are naked from the central pads to the toes—but the extent to which the area of the heel is covered with hair again varies even in species of the same genus.

Mungooses have no perfume glands—but all of them without exception have anal glands. The secretion of these glands is exuded into a sac or pouch from small openings on each side of or above the anus. The pouch itself surrounds and encloses the anal opening and might be mistaken for an enlarged anus. It is very large and conspicuous in such big species as the Stripe-necked Mungoose. It is less well developed in others and hardly noticeable in the small species of mungooses. The secretion of the anal glands is liquid, foul smelling and often copious. Mungooses have a habit of rubbing the glandular sac against objects in their path; hence it is inferred that one of the purposes of the glands is to leave behind a trail of scent and so familiarize the mungoose with every yard of its surroundings. It so becomes independent of vision and can find its way with precision over any road over which it has once travelled. Again many species of mungooses hunt in packs or family parties and such a trail of scent would help individuals to keep together. Finally one species, i.e. the Crab-eating Mungoose (*Herpestes urva*) is known to project or squirt the aqueous, horribly fetid contents of its anal sac to a great distance. It appears that this species at least makes use of the secretion as a means of defence. How far this habit is common to all Mungooses is not known.

The true Mungooses, those forming the genus *Herpestes*, are well known and familiar animals. They have long weasel-like bodies, and a more or less elongated tail bristling with long hairs. The longer hairs of the body are generally marked with alternate light and dark rings, which give a characteristic speckled or grizzled appearance to the fur. The head has a pointed muzzle with a rather short nose and the middle line of the upper lip is usually grooved. The object of this groove, which is seen in most Mungooses and in other carnivores is to help in the separation of the two halves of the upper lip when raised to clear the teeth. When the groove is obliterated the snout has to be raised to draw the lips away to bare the teeth.

Mungooses have a wide distribution ranging over the greater part of Africa, extending across the Straits of Gibraltar into Spain. Eastwards they are found through Southern Asia as far as the Islands of the Malay region. Of the many genera known, all, but one, are confined to Africa or Madagascar. The only genus found within our limits is *Herpestes* which includes the typical Mungooses. With the exception of the *Susicata* of South Africa —all the genera are included in a single sub-family *Herpestinae.*

Sub-family: *HERPESTINAE*.

THE COMMON MUNGOOSE (*HERPESTES EDWARDSI* GEOFF.).

The Common Indian Mungoose is found throughout the Peninsula of India from the Himalayas to Cape Comorin. It is said to occur in Assam, but it has not been observed in Burma. The Mungoose found in Ceylon is now considered a distinct species.

This species is so common and so frequently exhibited by itinerant snake-charmers, that it is familiar to all. The pattern of its somewhat long ragged fur is a coarse grizzle produced by the alternate dark and light rings on the hairs. The darker rings on the hairs may be almost black, or grey or some shade of brown, while the lighter rings are more or less white. The grizzling on the face, hands and feet is usually very fine; very coarse on the back and usually less obvious or absent on the under parts.

Various geographical races of the Common Mungoose are recognised and differentiated externally by the colouring of the face and feet, of the longer hairs of the body and the shorter under fur. The Common Mungoose (*H. edwardsi ferrugineus*) of Sind, Baluchistan and the more arid parts of the Northern Punjab, is so named because of the ruddy or ferruginous appearance of its head, feet and the tip of its tail. In the typical form (*H. e. edwardsi*) which is found in Nepal, Upper Bengal and Central India—the rusty colouring of these parts is much less pronounced. The annulations of the longer hairs are alternately brown and dirty white, and the under fur is sparse. Then there is a pale silvery coloured form, *H. e. pallens* which is found all over Rajputana. In this race the whole colouring is much lighter—a whitish silvery grey speckled with light brown, and the under fur is very dense and pure white. In the Common Mungoose of the Central Provinces and the Berars, *H. e. moerens*—the ferruginous wash on the face and feet is absent, the grizzling of the hairs is very pronounced, the black rings on the hairs contrasting strongly with the white; the under fur is creamy. In the South Indian race, *H. e. carnaticus*, which is found in Canara, Mysore, Coorg, the general colouring is dark steel grey, finely speckled with deep brown, giving the impression of a relatively dark coloured animal, the under fur is buff.

The Common Mungoose reaches a total length of nearly 3 ft. of which about 18 in. is tail. The average weight is about 3 lbs. Males are considerably larger and heavier than females.

The Mungoose lives in forest areas but is much commoner in cultivated country. It takes shelter under rocks and bushes, or digs a hole for itself in the ground, or uses the maze-like interior of a deserted termite mound, or a hole in the lower part of a tree trunk, or finds suitable shelter in the rafters of a house. Its food is varied. It preys upon rats and mice, snakes, lizards, frogs, insects, scorpions, centipedes, in brief on any creature that it can overcome and kill. It feeds on bird eggs and to a limited extent on vegetable matter. It will eat carrion and is frequently seen feeding on the kills of larger carnivores. It hunts by day and, when accustomed to Man, pays little regard to his presence. But in spite of excessive inquisitiveness, the mungoose is usually a wary creature, seldom straying far from cover. It can be very destructive, its destructiveness not being limited by its appetite. In a hen house or pigeon coop, a mungoose may achieve wholesale slaughter. Its prowess in killing snakes, rats and other vermin has earned the mungoose a world-wide reputation and has been the reason for its introduction into many countries—not always with the happiest of results. Many and remarkable are the descriptions of encounters between mungooses and snakes. Much has also been written about the supposed immunity of the mungoose to the poison of snakes. The prevalent belief throughout Oriental countries is that a mungoose when bitten seeks as an antidote a herb or root known in India as *Mangus wail* and on eating it, is rid of any harmful effects of snake poisoning. There is no truth in this belief. It is true that the mungoose is less sensitive to the venom and is able to withstand relatively large doses of poison, but its immunity is by no means absolute. A mungoose well and truly bitten and injected with venom sufficient to bring about its death will die like any other animal. All that can be said for it is, that in common with certain warm-blooded animals, like the pig or the hedgehog, it shows a certain resistance to the action of the venom. Cats for instance are less affected by it than dogs and pigs to a lesser extent than cats. Extreme agility in evading a bite gives the mungoose victory over the snake. When the snake strikes, the mungoose generally leaps aside to avoid the thrust and before the snake can recover to strike again, the animal rushes in, seizes and crushes its head with its sharp teeth. Other factors which avert an issue fatal to the mungoose are its tough skin which must be resistant to anything but a direct thrust and its habit of bristling the hairs of its body and tail under stress of excitement. It is suggested that with the hairs standing erect a mungoose looks twice as large as it really is and this must sometimes cause the snake to strike short.

Mungooses breed all the year round. The period of gestation is about sixty days. Three litters may be produced in a single year. A female kept in a semi-domesticated condition in Cannanore, South India, produced a litter of two in May, a second in September, a third in December and a fourth in June of the following year. The mother was in the habit of bringing her babies down from the roof when she came for her food. She climbed as well as a cat and was seen to jump a vertical height of over 4 ft. with a ten-days old baby in her mouth. When the young were able to follow her, she took them out on foraging expeditions. They kept close to her side, stopping when she stopped. The Common Mungoose is frequently seen hunting in couples or in family parties, the mother and the young are sometimes accompanied by a male.

The Mungoose makes a charming and docile pet. It is quite cleanly in its habit and has none of that unpleasant odour one usually finds in wild animals.

THE SMALL INDIAN MUNGOOSE (*HERPESTES AUROPUNCTATUS* HODGS.).

The Small Indian Mungoose is easily distinguished from the Common Mungoose by its small size and shorter and closer fur. It is restricted to the northern portion of India and is found along the lower slopes of the Himalayas from Sikhim to Kashmir and then across the plains from Baluchistan, Sind and the Punjab to Bengal. Southwards its range extends into Rajputana, Gwalior, Gujerat and Kathiawar.

The Small Mungoose is from 18 to 22 in. in total length. Its general colouring ranges from a speckled greyish to golden yellow or to brown. The form found in Baluchistan and Sind, known as *H. a. pallipes*, is distinguished by its pale grey colouring. *H. a. helvus* which is found in Kathiawar, Gujerat and Gwalior is a more yellow in general colour. The forehead is a deep yellow buff—the feet light yellow, the underside paler and the general colour yellow grey minutely speckled with brown. In the typical form found along the Himalayas and in Behar and Bengal, the general colouring is brown, minutely speckled with yellow. In Assam, Manipur and Burma, the Indian species is replaced by another form known as the Small Burmese Mungoose (*H. birmanicus*) which is still darker in colouring and markedly larger in size. Reference must also be made to a third species described under the name of *H. nipalensis*, distinguished from *H. auropunctatus* by the much finer grizzling and generally darker colouration of its coat. It has been taken at a level of 7,000 ft. in Nepal and in Midnapur in Bengal. It is a rare and little known species.

The Small Mungoose lives and breeds in holes apparently burrowed by itself. It is diurnal in habit and is seen about bushes, hedges and cultivated fields. It is a cautious creature generally keeping to cover. Its presence can usually be detected by the worn tracks it leaves along hedges. It feeds on anything that it can kill, on rats and mice, snakes, scorpions, centipedes, wasps and insects of all kinds—as such, like its larger relative it is useful in ridding a house of vermin. Like the Common Mungoose it makes a useful and charming pet but is apparently less certain in temper. A tame female kept in a semi-wild state paired with a wild male on the 4th of July and on the night of the 23rd August after a period of seven weeks produced a litter of three young—one male and two females. Her second litter of two, both females was produced on the 14th April and on the 9th July she produced two more, both females. The newly-born young are described as being remarkably ugly, practically hairless and of a dark mouse colour. The eyes opened on the 16th-17th day after birth. When suckling they purred like a cat. The mother gave vent to a purring sound whenever she was given a drink of milk. She was most restless and for the first two or three weeks would constantly move her offspring from place to place carrying them as a cat carries her kitten. While her young were helpless she was very savage in their defence.

THE RUDDY MUNGOOSE (*HERPESTES SMITHII* GRAY)

The Ruddy Mungoose is a species which is mainly restricted to forest areas. Its range extends from Rajputana, Central and Western India, southward to Ceylon. The species attains a length of approximately 3 ft. of which **1 ft.** 6 in. is tail.

The general colouring of the animal is a iron grey, produced by the white, grey and brown rings of its hairs which are tipped with rusty brown. The head and legs are washed with reddish brown and the feet are almost black. This species is easily distinguished from the Common Mungoose by the black tip to its tail. There is however a wide range of variation in colouring which has led to the recognition of six more or less distinct geographical races. The typical form is found in Central and Western India from Hoshangabad southwards to the Nilgiris. The general colour is dark with less rufous, the legs are not conspicuously reddish though the ankles often are. The form found in North-East Rajputana, *H. s. rusanus*, is similar to the typical race in colouring but it is a small animal representing the extreme in the gradual reduction in size from south to north. A third race, *H. s. caneus*, is described from Mount Abu, South-West Rajputana—the general colouring is a clear grizzled grey without the brownish or rufous characteristic of the other races. The form found in the Eastern Ghats, *H. s. jerdoni*, is drabbish grey. The Ceylon form, *H. s. zeylanicus*, is the largest and most richly coloured of all—the whole colouring being richly rufous.

In Mount Abu this species is fairly common. It lives in burrows and shelters among rocks. Family parties have been observed hunting by day. Its food is probably similar to that of other mungooses. Being a creature of forest area it is less commonly observed and nothing is recorded about its breeding habits.

THE NILGIRI BROWN MUNGOOSE (*HERPESTES FUSCUS* WATERHOUSE).

The Nilgiri Brown Mungoose is restricted to the hill forests of the Nilgiris, Palnis, Travancore and Coorg and possibly other hill ranges of South-Western India.

It is a large heavily-built blackish brown mungoose more or less speckled with yellow or brownish white. The paws are almost black. The under fur is brown—the longer hairs of the body have alternate rings of blackish brown and yellow or yellowish white, three or four of each, the darker rings are much wider than the light. The head and body of this mungoose measure about 19 in., the tail 12 in.; the weight of a male is about 6 lbs.

This mungoose is fairly common in the coffee plantations. Nothing has been recorded about its breeding habits.

THE STRIPE-NECKED MUNGOOSE (*HERPESTES VITTICOLLIS* BENNETT).

This Stripe-necked Mungoose, the largest of all Asiatic Mungooses, is found in the hill ranges of South-Western India, from Kanara southward to Ceylon. It is a very handsome creature with an iron grey head, the body speckled with brown, yellow and red. On the lower part of the back and tail there is a profusion of long chestnut hairs. A very distinctive black stripe marks each side of the neck. The end of the tail is black. In life the shape of the head differs from that of the Common Mungoose (*H. edwardsi*), the snout having a slightly upward curve. This mungoose grows to over 3 ft. in length and weighs about 7 lbs.

This species is common all over the Nilgiri and Palni plateaux and is equally abundant in the swamps and rice fields of the Wynaad. Unlike other Indian mungooses it appears to be less plentiful in the neighbourhood of human habitations. Large and powerfully built, these mungooses can be very destructive to game —they hunt a good deal by day and are seen prowling about frequently in couples—presumably following their quarry by scent and then burrowing for it in the ground. These large mungooses have extraordinary tough skins and with their wiry hair are almost proof against dog bites.

Nothing is known about their breeding habits.

THE CRAB-EATING MUNGOOSE (*HERPESTES URVA* HODGSON).

The Crab-eating Mungoose is found at low elevations in the South-Eastern Himalayas, in Assam. Its range extends into Burma, Tenasserim and Southern China.

Like the Stripe-necked Mungoose it is a large and powerfully built creature. The general colouring of its coarse and ragged fur is a dusky iron grey with a greyish surface caused by the long whitish tips to the hairs. A well marked, narrow white stripe runs along each side of the neck from the angle of the mouth to the shoulder. The head is dark brown speckled with white, the legs are similar in colour, but there is no white speckling on the feet. They are usually black. In this species the soles of the hind feet are naked only for about two-thirds of their length, the heel area being covered with hair. The woolly under fur is dark brown at the base then pale brownish yellow. The dimensions of this mungoose are as follows:—Head and body 18-21 in., tail without hair at the end 10-12 in. Unlike other species, the Crab-eating Mungoose is mainly aquatic. It lives on the banks of rivers and streams and preys mainly on frogs, crabs and fishes. A specimen was shot on the Chindwin River while burrowing in a bank. In Kurseong one of these mungooses came repeatedly to a tank stocked with Gold Fish—it took many of the fish and must have dived from the tank side to procure them.

Nothing is known of its breeding habits.

FAMILY: IV *HYAENIDAE*: HYAENAS.

Hyaenas resemble dogs rather than cats in external build, and may be easily taken for members of the Dog-tribe. Structural details of the skull and the character of the teeth however definitely place the Hyaenas within the Aeluroid or Cat Section of the Carnivores.

The closest relatives of the Hyaenas are believed to be the Civets and Mungooses. Some authors trace a particular affinity between hyaenas and mungooses—both groups of animals having certain points of structure in common. The relationship between hyaenas and civets and their kindred is not very apparent in existing species, but it is more strikingly revealed in the structure of extinct forms which lived during past geological epochs. In the lower part of the Pliocene there occurs an interesting civet-like animal known as the Ictithere which in its structure serves to reveal a close alliance between these two families of Carnivores.

During past epochs, hyaenas inhabited the greater part of Europe and ranged in Asia as far east as China. Fossil species are numerous. No less than 5 different species have been found in the Siwalik fossil beds of the Punjab. One of these extinct forms from Northern India, in the length of its jaws and in the form and number of its teeth makes a close approach to the civets. The teeth of the present day hyaenas are in some respects feline in character and differ in these points from the teeth of civets. A hyaena has 34 teeth in its jaws, a cat 30 and a civet usually 44. The numerical difference in the teeth of cats and hyaenas is accounted for by the retention in the Hyaena of an additional premolar tooth, on each side, both in the upper and lower jaws. A hyaena has 4 premolars and 1 molar on each side in its upper jaw, and 3 premolars and 1 molar in the lower. As in Cats, the molar, the last tooth in a hyaena's upper jaw is reduced to a minute tooth. All the cheek teeth in the lower jaw are conical teeth with sharp cutting blades. But the distinctiveness of the Hyaena's dentition is seen in the great size and strength of the cheek teeth as compared with the canines; more specially in the massive conical crowns of the second and third premolars in both jaws. These teeth carry a strongly pronounced basal ridge which acts as a shield for protecting the gums. This form of tooth is especially designed for gnawing and breaking bones. The teeth and jaws of hyaenas have assumed those characters which adapt them for their peculiar food and habits. The Hyaena is a scavenger. It feeds on the bones and the coarser remains left over by beasts of prey. The whole skull has its shape modified by the enormous development of the muscles which work the jaws and teeth. Few Carnivores have jaws and teeth which can compare in strength or bone crushing power with those of hyaenas.

The Hyaena is a massively built animal with broad short head and a deep body. Its legs are comparatively long—particularly the fore limbs, so that the hind quarters droop. The massive build of the fore part of the body as compared with the hind, and its knock-kneed hind legs gives the hyaena an awkward, hang-dog appearance. The hair is coarse and shaggy. The thickness of the coat, the colour and the boldness of the markings appear to vary with season.

A hyaena has only 4 toes on its fore and hind feet, the digits corresponding to the thumb and the big toe are absent. The claws are short and blunt, they are unprotected with sheaths and are non-retractile. The feet differ in some respects from the feet of cats or civets. The pads under the toes show several peculiarities. The bases of the toe pads are set at right angles to the central or the plantar pad of the sole. Again the pads are not elliptical but more or less conical in shape. In the uptilting of the toe pads, in their rigidity, compactness, and shape as well as in the short blunt claws the feet of hyaenas resemble those of dogs. The toe pads of cats and civets are usually elliptical in form, and their bases lie in the same plane as the plantar pads of the sole. Hyaenas have anal glands which exude their secretion into a pouch. The presence of an anal pouch in hyaenas and mungooses is cited as part of the evidence of affinity between these two animals. But Pocock has indicated the considerable difference between the anal pouches in the two groups. In mungooses the anus opens in the centre of the anal pouch and the margins of the pouch close right over the anus, also the orifices of the glands are situated tolerably near the anus. In the hyaenas on the other hand, the opening of the pouch appears as a curved slit over the anus, the orifice of the glands are far removed from it.

The existing species of hyaenas are three in number. All of them are included in the genus *Hyaena*. Only one species the Striped Hyaena is found within our limits and extends its range into Africa. The Brown Hyaena (*H. bruneus*) and the Spotted Hyaena (*H. crocuta*) are now limited to Africa. Fossil remains of the Spotted Hyaena have been excavated from some caves near Kurnool in the Madras Presidency, indicating the past existence of this species in India.

THE STRIPED HYAENA (*HYAENA HYAENA* LINN.).

The Striped Hyaena is found throughout the Peninsula of India. It is not found in Ceylon nor in the countries to the east of the Bay of Bengal. In the west its range extends through South-Western Asia into East and North-West Africa. During and before the age of the Mammoth, the Striped Hyaena inhabited a considerable part of Europe. Its bones have been discovered in a cave in the south of France, and teeth of this species have been found in England.

The colour and markings of the hyaena vary considerably with season. Much depends on whether the animal is in fresh coat or has shed its hairs or whether it is in its fuller winter coat. Various races of this animal have been described without any account being taken of these factors. Linnaeus originally gave the name *hyaena* to a hyaena from South Persia. The Persian animal is believed to be similar to the Indian, but if the Indian form is proved to be distinct, it will carry the name *H. h. indica* Blainville.

The Indian Hyaena does not develop a very long winter coat; but it is full, much fuller than the hot weather coat and comparatively soft. The colouring is cream or buffy white and the head tawny buff—the whole colour tone changes to grey or dirty white in the harsher and scantier summer coat. The transverse stripes fade from black to brown—they may be less evident in the fuller winter coat or again tend to become obliterated in cases where the subsequent shedding of the hairs leave the flanks of the animal almost bare.

The Striped Hyaena stands about 3 ft. high at the shoulders—the head and body of a male measures a little over 3½ ft. and the tail with terminal hairs is about 1½ ft. in length. A good-sized female may scale 75 lbs.—the male is about 10 lbs. heavier. Hyaenas are more common in the drier parts of India—particularly among rocky hills or nullahs—or by the outskirts of jungles in the plains. They are found in the open areas of the Nilgiris around and above Ootacamund at elevations ranging from 3,000 to 8,000 ft. They usually shelter in caves, or among boulders, and frequently make a den in an enlarged porcupine's earth. Hyaenas are nocturnal in habit coming out in quest of food about sunset and retiring before sunrise. They usually go about in pairs—parties of five or six have been seen together, but this is unusual with this species. They are great wanderers and their tracks are quite common. The foot print is much like that of a dog—except that the print of the fore foot is much larger than the hind. The pug is easily differentiated from that of a panther by the print of the claws.

The hyaena is mainly a scavenger, and as such performs a useful task. It feeds on the carcases of animals that have died of disease or been killed by other beasts of prey. The carcase is eaten where it lies but portions of it may be carried off into the animal's den. Hyaenas sometimes kill and carry off sheep and goats. They are particularly partial to dogs. They do not usually attack larger cattle. There is a record of two cows, tied up as a bait for tiger being killed by a hyaena. The stomachs of the animals were ripped open and they were literally eaten into when yet alive. It is recorded that this species is far more aggressive in Africa than it is in India and that, in Abyssinia, Striped Hyaenas have developed a habit of killing sheep and goats and frequently run amock in a flock killing a dozen or more animals. Fortunately in India our hyaena can in no sense be considered aggressive, despite its bulk and power, it does not attack larger animals, though individuals may be quite prepared, if need be, to appropriate and dispute the kills of panthers or even tigers. There are several instances on record of hyaenas depriving panthers of their kills and of routing them in disputes.

While hunger may give the hyaena inordinate courage, when brought to bay, it does not show fight. Dunbar Brander states it will frequently sham death when harried by a pack of dogs, submitting passively to the direst worrying and ill-treatment.

Though not usually very demonstrative hyaenas give vent to various weird noises, a common sound is a loud laughing chatter.

Little is known about the breeding habits of hyaenas, it is recorded that in the Central Provinces they breed during the cold weather and that the young are generally born in the hot weather —5-6 being produced in a litter.

When taken young, hyaenas are easily tamed and make very affectionate and docile pets.